INSTITUTE FOR PUBLIC POLICY RESEARCH

Accountable Policing

Effectiveness, Empowerment and Equity

Edited by Robert Reiner
and Sarah Spencer

CONTENTS

page

NOTES ON CONTRIBUTORS

Barry Loveday is a Principal Lecturer at the University of Central England and has worked in the Police Department at the Home Office. His publications include a research report on Merseyside Police Authority (1985), 'The Future Structure of Police Forces' in *Public Money and Management* (1992), 'Police and Government in the 1990s' in *Social Policy and Administration* (Winter 1991) and 'Police Authorities in the 1990s' in *Political Quarterly*, 1991.

Robert Reiner is Professor of Criminology at the London School of Economics. He is the author of many books on policing including *The Politics of the Police* (Wheatsheaf, 1985, 2nd ed. 1992) and *Chief Constables* (OUP 1991). He is co-editor of *Policing and Society: an International Journal of Research and Policy* and review editor of *The British Journal of Criminology*.

Andrew Sanders is a Senior Lecturer in Law and Fellow of Pembroke College, Oxford. He is co-author (with Mike McConville and Roger Leng) of *The Case for the Prosecution* (Routledge 1991) and co-author (with Lee Bridges) of *Advice and Assistance at Police Stations* published by the Lord Chancellor's Department in 1989. He has been a member of the Parole Board since 1990.

Sarah Spencer is a Research Fellow at IPPR and a former General Secretary of the National Council for Civil Liberties. Her publications include *Called to Account: Police Accountability in England and Wales* (NCCL 1985) and *Police Authorities during the Miners' Strike* (Cobden Trust, 1985). She co-ordinated IPPR's project on the UK constitution which led to *A British Bill of Rights* (1990) and *The Constitution of the United Kingdom* (1991) and is editor of a forthcoming report on UK immigration and refugee policy.

Neil Walker is a Senior Lecturer in Public Law at the University of Edinburgh. He has researched and published on many areas of public law and policy including local-central relations, freedom of expression and police decision-making and accountability. Publications in the field of police studies include *Managing the Police* (Wheatsheaf, 1986, with D.Bradley and R.Wilkie) and *The UK Police and European Co-operation* (Edinburgh University, 1991).

Mollie Weatheritt was, at the time of writing, Deputy Director of The Police Foundation. She previously worked in the Home Office Research and Planning Unit and from 1978 to 1981 was research secretary to the Royal Commission on Criminal Procedure. Her publications include *Innovations in Policing* (Croom Helm, 1986) and *The Future of Police Research* (Avebury, 1989).

ACKNOWLEDGEMENTS

IPPR would like to thank Simon James for the discussion paper which he contributed in the early stages of this project and those who attended the seminar in January 1991 at which it was discussed. We should also like to thank those who attended the seminar in December 1992 to discuss drafts of the papers which are published in this volume.

PREFACE

The sea-change in the management of Britain's public services is to culminate in a new legislative framework for the management of the police service. Recognising, in the then Home Secretary's words, that 'organisations are better run when responsibility is devolved to local managers', central control over the allocation of force expenditure is to be devolved to local police chiefs and their police authority. Local authorities, however, will effectively lose their residual influence over policing while continuing to pay part of the bill. Police authorities will become free standing committees with half of their members non-elected magistrates and central government nominees. Central control will be reinforced by the Home Secretary's powers to appoint each authority's chairman and to set national performance targets which police authorities will be required to attain. Police authorities will, within those limits, be expected to set local objectives and performance targets. While chief constables retain 'direction and control' of their forces, however, it is not clear what power they will have to ensure that those targets are attained.

Months before the Home Secretary announced these proposals in March 1993[1], IPPR decided to review the structure of police decision making. Much had happened since police accountability, defined narrowly in terms of the powers of police authorities, had been widely discussed in the early 1980s: the internal accountability of the police had been strengthened by setting objectives and monitoring performance; the influence of central government had been substantially enhanced, largely at the expense of local police authorities, the most radical of which had been abolished; the trend towards operational decisions at a regional and national level had accelerated, while decisions on local service delivery were gradually delegated down to local command units; there had been a growing involvement of senior officers in European and international initiatives for which neither government policy nor the eventual objectives were clear; and the government had initiated a review of local government structure with major implications for police authorities. Last, but not least, confidence in the police and the criminal justice system had been dented by a series of wrongful convictions, leading to the establishment of a Royal Commission on Criminal Justice.

In initiating our own review, we had an open mind on the conclusions it might reach but not on some underlying principles. The first of these was that the nature of the police service, while different in some important respects from other public services, requires no less accountability to elected representatives for the way in which the service is carried out. We do not see policing as primarily a matter of neutral or technical expertise, nor simply as the delivery of a necessary social service. It is, as Robert Reiner puts it, about the regulation of social conflict and the representation of social authority, and disputes about the way in which it is carried out are always, in part, questions of politics.

Secondly, because of the potential for the abuse of this service, we are convinced that local government should, like central government, play a significant part in police decision making, informed by the expertise and experience of police officers. We are concerned at the drift towards central control and mindful of the importance of local public support to police effectiveness. Thus we looked to ways to reverse this trend. In relation to those few aspects of police work requiring national co-ordination, we have concluded that it is not possible to do so. But we do not share the former Home Secretary's distrust of local government nor his view that it is an inappropriate body to manage a public service. There is however scope for improvement in how that responsibility is exercised and on this we have made some recommendations.

Thirdly, we were aware that our aim must be to devise a system which achieves meaningful accountability and not merely the formal trappings, a system which influences the working practices of the organisation and not just the formal rules; that is, a process which enlists the support of the police themselves. The framework for police accountability in a democratic society must be adequate both in principle and in practice.

In contrast to earlier writing on police accountability, we have not sought to make a separation between the operational decisions of individual officers and policy decisions. Rather, we have looked at the underlying principles according to which decisions should be taken by officials or by elected representatives and then suggested ways in which accountability for particular kinds of decision could be enhanced. The areas of decision making covered extend from those of the constable on the street (Andrew Sanders) through police authorities (Barry Loveday) to international policy making fora (Neil Walker). Mollie Weatheritt examines the issues raised by the new emphasis on performance measurement while Robert Reiner sets the agenda, examining the recent historical background, the key issues and fundamental principles. Together, he and I draw up the principal conclusions (with which each of the other contributors may not always concur). A summary of the recommendations concludes that final chapter.

During the course of our discussions we held a seminar attended by senior police officers, representatives from the Home Office, Audit Commission, Sheehy Enquiry, local government, academia and organisations advising those at the sharp end of policing decisions. Their comments were invaluable to us in revising our ideas. Our thanks are due to the Barrow and Geraldine S Cadbury Trust for supporting that event.

Publication of our report now coincides with the consultation period on the Government's proposals. The appointment of a new Home Secretary in May has added to the uncertainty about the final form which the legislative proposals will take. We hope that this report will assist those reflecting on the proposed reforms and encourage them to consider, in some instances, adopting a very different course.

Sarah Spencer
June 1993

1. Statement on the Police by the Home Secretary, House of Commons, 23 March 1993 col 765.

1. POLICE ACCOUNTABILITY: PRINCIPLES, PATTERNS AND PRACTICES
Robert Reiner

Police accountability is one of the thorniest conundrums of statecraft, as Juvenal's famous question *'Quis custodiet ipsos custodes'* conveyed nearly two millennia ago. Guarding the guardian poses peculiarly problematic issues both of principle and practice, particularly in a democratic society. The police are the specialist carriers of the state's bedrock power : the monopoly of legitimate force. How and for what this is used speaks to the very heart of the condition of a political order. The dangers of abuse, on behalf of particular partisan interests or the police themselves, are clear and daunting.

Fears of this kind were expressed by the diverse groups who opposed the initial creation of modern police forces in Britain, in the late eighteenth and early nineteenth centuries. Since then concerns about the direction and control of the powers vested in the police have surfaced regularly at times of political tension. During the late 1970s and early 1980s political and social polarisation increased greatly in Britain, and the police became embroiled in acute controversies (Reiner, 1992). Whether the police were adequately accountable became a prominent issue (Morgan and Smith, 1989). In recent years partisan conflict over police accountability has abated. But great concerns about policing remain and these necessarily raise questions of how the police are to be controlled and managed.

The Emergence of the Accountability Issue

The foundation text for the present structure of police accountability is the Police Act 1964. This was rooted in but not identical with recommendations of the Royal Commission on the Police which had been established in 1959 and reported in 1962. The Royal Commission had been set up in response to a number of scandals in the late 1950s which raised questions about the structure of accountability which existed then. Several of these cases involved allegations of malpractice and corruption on the part of police officers, including two chief constables. Another case concerned interference by the Nottingham Watch Committee with an investigation into alleged corruption amongst local councillors. When the Chief Constable, Captain Popkess, refused to provide them with information on the progress of the investigation, the Watch Committee suspended him. The Home Secretary instructed the Committee to reinstate Popkess, but this case together with the others indicated a need to clarify the respective roles of local police authorities, chief constables, and the Secretary of State. This issue was at the heart of the Royal Commission's deliberations, as was the question of constructing adequate means of redress in individual cases where police were accused of malpractice.

The Police Act of 1964 established the present formal structure of governance for police forces and the elements of the system for handling complaints against the police. For provincial forces (of which there are now 41) the Act specifies what is usually referred to as the tripartite system of police governance. Under this, responsibility for policing is divided between local police authorities (one-third of the members of which are Justices of the Peace, and two-thirds local councillors), chief constables, and the Home Secretary. The two London forces remain *sui generis*. The City of London Police have as a local police authority the Common Council of the City of London (the Lord Mayor and the Alderman). The Metropolitan Police - by far the country's largest and most influential - has no local police authority at all. Its police authority is the Home Secretary. On 23 March 1993, Mr Kenneth Clarke announced proposals to end this 160 year old anomaly and establish a local police authority for London. However he also announced plans to secure effective central control over *all* local police authorities, by reducing the locally elected proportion of their members to 50 per cent. The other 50 per cent would be centrally appointed, some directly by the Home Secretary, whilst others would continue to be JPs (who are selected by the Lord Chancellor). The Home Secretary would choose the chair of the police authority.

The system for dealing with complaints against the police which the 1964 Police Act (s. 49) set up imposed for the first time a duty on the police to record and investigate all complaints against themselves. More serious complaints were to be investigated by officers from outside the division or even the force of the complained against officer. However, the system lacked any independent element in the investigation and adjudication of complaints.

Both the governance and the complaints mechanisms laid down by the 1964 Act attracted a degree of contemporary criticism from academic commentators, civil liberties groups and some politicians and lawyers. However, as the police became increasingly involved in controversy during the 1970s, with the growth of public disorder in a variety contexts, rapidly rising crime, and mounting racial tension, so concern about the inadequacy of the accountability arrangements grew.

Dissatisfaction with the way complaints were handled, especially the fact that there was no independent element involved in their investigation and adjudication, surfaced regularly when there were revelations of police malpractice. In 1976 this led to another Police Act which introduced an independent Police Complaints Board. This Board received copies of the investigating officer's report on any complaint under s.49 of the 1964 Act, together with the deputy chief constable's decision as to whether to bring disciplinary charges or not. The Board had the power to recommend a disciplinary tribunal should be set up on which it would constitute the majority. However, as its sole source of information was the case constructed by the police investigators it is hardly surprising that the Board seldom countermanded the police decision.

Pressure to include an independent element in the *investigation* as well as in the adjudication of complaints continued. In 1981 even the Police Federation joined the clamour of voices calling for a completely independent system, which it saw as the price of restoring public confidence. Eventually in the Police and Criminal Evidence Act (PACE) 1984 the government replaced the Police

Complaints Board with the Police Complaints Authority (PCA). The PCA took on the same *post hoc* review and adjudication functions as the old Board had; but it also acquired the power to supervise the police investigation of any complaints which it wanted to follow and it was required to supervise certain types of serious complaint investigations, notably alleged assaults by police. A system of informal resolution of non-serious complaints, subject to the agreement of the complainant and the complained-against officer, was also set up. This was intended to eliminate the need for the whole panoply of the formal complaints process in minor cases, and to allow the PCA's capacity to be preserved for the major ones. Although the evidence suggests that the PCA does its work as committedly and thoroughly as its resources permit, it is also clear from research on public opinion that the new system commands no more confidence than the old one (Maguire and Corbett 1991). Therefore there remains strong demand from critics, including the Police Federation, for a completely independent system.

Outside the ranks of a few academics and dedicated police watchers there was little concern about the tripartite system of police governance until the late 1970s. 1981 marked a turning-point in this, as in so many other aspects of policing. In May 1981 radical Labour councils were elected in all the Metropolitan areas (including the Greater London Council - GLC). These provided a power base for the growing critical questioning of police strategies and practices to find significant expression. Between 1981 and 1985 there were numerous clashes between these authorities and their chief constables, most notably in Manchester and Merseyside. The Local Government Act 1985 abolished these radical authorities, replacing them with joint boards which have proved more open to police influence (Loveday 1991). This, together with the Labour Party's growing new realism largely pushed the issue of achieving greater accountability of police policies to local authorities off the political stage.

The issue of accountability has far from disappeared, however. The Police and Criminal Evidence Act 1984 (PACE) attempts to provide a framework for the much tighter regulation of police powers, through the police disciplinary process. The problem of making officers accountable for the use of their powers in specific cases has become even more critical since the flood of miscarriage of justice scandals since 1989 when the Guildford Four were finally released after a successful appeal. This, together with other later cases, notably the Birmingham Six and Tottenham Three, aroused much disquiet and prompted the establishment in 1991 of the Royal Commission on Criminal Justice chaired by Lord Runciman, the first to be appointed since the Conservatives came to power in 1979.

Two more recent developments have highlighted facets of police accountability which had not been prominent in earlier debates. A central feature of the Conservative government's economic strategy has been the control of public expenditure. In 1983 Home Office Circular 114 applied the Government's Financial Management Initiative to the police service. Since then (with a temporary hiatus during the Miners' Strike of 1984-5) there has been a steady tightening of financial and managerial accountability within the police service. The role of H.M. Inspectorate of Constabulary (HMIC) in monitoring police efficiency (through an annual inspection to assess fitness to receive central government funding) has been enhanced considerably. Inspections are much more searching and rigorous and a vast quantity of detailed information has to be provided which is analysed in terms of the Inspectorate's Matrix of Performance Indicators. The search for value for money in the police service has also been joined by the Audit Commission and National Audit Office, with responsibilities for monitoring local and central government financial management respectively.

Police senior management is thus much more rigorously called to account now for its efficient, effective and economical use of resources by these governmental bodies. In turn there is an attempt at more systematic monitoring and appraisal of performance through the internal management system. In 1992, the Home Office established the Sheehy Inquiry Into Police Roles, Ranks, Responsibilities and Rewards to examine police organisation for ways of enhancing efficient management, and it is due to report in June 1993. Thus, whilst local democratic accountability has declined

both in substance and as a political issue, police accountability to
the law for the use of their legal powers, and to internal
management systems for efficient use of resources, has been
enhanced, and are the subject of major inquiries at present.

A final factor in the emergence of new accountability concerns is
the growing involvement of British policing in co-operation with
foreign forces. Most important of all are the implications of
European integration for the police. Greater crime of a cross-border
kind is feared and this has led to the proliferation of international
agreements for co-operation and exchange of information. This
internationalisation of policing clearly raises profound questions of
accountability. To whom and how are police accountable when
involved in joint work with other countries? How is the use of
information controlled?

Police Accountability: Back to the Basics

The police exercise powers which profoundly affect the lives of all
citizens. In a democracy it is expected that those who wield public
power must be fully accountable for this. The first step in designing
an adequate structure of accountability for the police must be to go
back to basics. *What type* of decisions do the police make, explicitly
and implicitly, in exercising their powers? *To whom* should they be
accountable for the different sorts of decisions? *What type* of
accountability should they have to the relevant bodies? *What
mechanisms* should be established to deliver effectively the
appropriate type of accountability to such bodies? I will review
these fundamental issues of principle in this chapter; later chapters
will explore each facet in more detail before we offer a set of
recommendations in the conclusion.

Types of police decision-making

A fundamental distinction must be made between two classes of
police decision. General policy decisions are ones which do not
relate to specific individual cases. They may comprise decisions
about internal organisational matters, or about desirable objectives

or styles of law enforcement. On the other hand, individual officers will also continuously be making decisions about how to exercise (or refrain from exercising) their powers in specific cases.

This distinction appears to correspond to the distinction between policy and operational matters which, although not written into the 1964 Police Act itself, has been widely assumed to demarcate the specific roles of police authorities and chief constables respectively. The policy versus operations distinction has been criticised cogently by several commentators, notably Laurence Lustgarten who demonstrates that it is false and untenable in the final analysis (Lustgarten 1986, pp. 20-2).

All policy decisions, even when they appear to be far removed from specific operations, have a potential impact upon them. Purely domestic issues, for instance the style of catering in the police canteen, have implications for morale and hence effectiveness (not to speak of consequences for the 'canteen culture' which is the immediate source of constables' decisions on the streets). For example, in a highly publicised clash with his police authority in 1984, Greater Manchester's then Chief Constable Sir James Anderton, objected to the committee's proposal to disband the police band, on the ground that it infringed his operational autonomy. Whilst the police authority was legally advised that the question of how much money to allocate to the band was within its power, Anderton claimed that he had been legally advised that it was not. The issue was not tested in the courts, as on this occasion the chief constable backed down in order 'to maintain a good relationship between the committee and myself'. However, it illustrates the difficulty in making any absolute distinction between policy and operational questions. On the other hand, the sum of specific decisions in individual operations amounts to a *de facto* policy about how to deal with such cases, even if it is never explicitly articulated as such.

Whilst there can be no valid distinction between policy and operational matters as two hermetically sealed classes of decision, there is a contrast between decisions made by officers about specific cases or individual operations, and decisions about general issues. Whilst the balance of decisions made by officers at different levels in the rank structure will vary, they will all make some decisions of both kinds. Thus, senior officers will primarily be making decisions of a general policy kind, but they may occasionally be involved in specific operations of sufficient significance, a common example of which is being appointed the investigating officer in cases of serious complaints in other forces. In my interviews with chief constables I was told of several occasions when they had made arrests themselves, even dressed in formal dinner-suits *en route* to official functions (Reiner 1991, pp. 160-64, p. 330). Middle management will regularly be involved in both types of decision.

Whilst street-level officers would not be responsible explicitly for general policy decisions, the way they exercise their discretion in specific cases, when aggregated with other similar decisions, constitutes the *de facto* working rules of the police organisation. As has been commonly remarked in the research literature, these may deviate from the formal organisational policies. The paradoxical consequence is that the most important policy decisions in terms of impact upon citizens are determined implicitly by the lowest ranks in the formal organisational hierarchy. A major problem in constructing adequate institutions of police accountability is that the decisions which ultimately have the greatest effect on ordinary people are low visibility ones, made day-by-day by constables on the streets and in the backstage areas of police stations.

An important feature of command level police decisions must also be noted. It follows partly from the inevitable fact of the low visibility, dispersed nature of routine, everyday police work. But it stems more directly from the way that the English legal tradition regards the office of constable. A long line of cases has repeatedly stressed that the constable holds an independent office under the Crown and is responsible only to the law and not to his or her organisational superiors (nor any external governmental agency) for the way that s/he exercises his or her powers. As long as the decisions are lawful (ie. neither corrupt, an abuse of authority, nor a total abnegation of law enforcement responsibility) no body can over-ride the constable's judgement about the best method of enforcing the law. This applies alike to the judgement of rank-and-file officers at the scene of potential offenses about when there is sufficient evidence to justify legal intervention[1] or the general policy decisions of senior officers about the procedures to follow in a particular type of incident[2] so long as there is no decision *never* to enforce the law at all in a whole class of cases.

The implication of this vaunted legal doctrine of constabulary independence is that there is a distinction between two types of general policy decision, organisational and law enforcement ones. Decisions are made in a mandatory way only when they relate to internal organisational procedures, although these will have implications that structure the pattern of law enforcement in specific cases. Only internal organisational matters will be the subject of policy decisions in the strict sense, ie. where a clear line of conduct is unequivocally sanctioned (Grimshaw and Jefferson 1987). Such decisions may range all the way from one to buy British cars, through the establishment of specialist squads, to instructions to radio in to headquarters before pursuing fleeing getaway cars into particular areas (the policy involved in the *ex. p. Levey* case). Whilst these types of decision will have implications, more or less directly, for specific cases, they are not explicitly about what the outcome should be in any particular incident.

Policies which explicitly concern law enforcement as distinct from organisational questions will be couched in advisory rather than mandatory style, eg. Scarman's famous principle that the preservation of public tranquillity is of greater importance than strict law enforcement. The ultimate decision about how such general policies should be interpreted in particular concrete circumstances is always left to individual constables. They may receive more or less strictly phrased, more or less unambiguous, guidance - but the final discretion still rests with them. Whilst it is inevitable logically that the constables on the scene have some *de facto* discretion about what the best course of action is in particular situations, it does not follow that their exercise of judgement should not be reviewable and sanctionable after the event, not only for impropriety but whether it was the most sensible decision. That constables' decisions are unreviewable is a policy decision of English law which has protected a strict notion of constabulary independence. The wisdom of this is highly debatable.

Decisions made by the police thus vary along two dimensions. Do they relate to a general type of case, or to specific concrete incidents? Do they concern internal organisational matters or law enforcement? Putting these two dimensions together yields the following typology of police decision-making. Each type has very different implications for accountability, which must be considered.

Figure 1: Types of Police Decision

	General Policy	Individual Cases
Law Enforcement	*(a) Policing Styles*	*(b) Use of Legal Powers*
Internal Organisation	*(c) House-keeping*	*(d) Personnel Management*

a. Policing Styles

By a style of policing I mean a policy about how a whole category of incidents is dealt with. The actual style of policing in an area results from the myriad decisions made in concrete encounters by individual officers. However, policies will often be formulated by senior officers which aim to tip this in particular directions. For example, during the 1980s there developed a general concern about the way domestic violence was dealt with by the police. Responding to a variety of pressures, senior officers wanted to ensure that such cases were taken more seriously. One straightforward way of achieving this would be the kind of mandatory arrest policies which have been adopted in several North American forces (with debatable results). However, to issue an order requiring arrest in all cases of alleged domestic assault would run contrary to the constabulary independence doctrine. Instead forces have adopted a variety of measures intended to encourage arrest in suitable cases, but without making it mandatory.

Command level decisions aimed at influencing policing styles are necessarily explicitly formulated by senor officers and they can in principle be made accountable to external agencies for them. The difficulty is that they bear a problematic relationship to the *de facto* pattern of law enforcement decisions on the ground. The constabulary independence doctrine inhibits the formulation of law enforcement policies which are mandatory rather than exhortatory. Even if they were couched in directive rather than permissive fashion, however, an element of discretion inevitably would remain for constables on the ground. Decisions *not* to enforce the law are especially hard to review as no record of the encounter may be made and there will often be no witnesses apart from police and suspects.

b. The Use of Legal Powers

As argued above, decisions *not* to use legal powers pose particular problems for accountability. Decisions *to* invoke legal powers, eg. to stop and search or arrest or detain in custody or charge a suspect, necessarily result in some formal records. The use of legal powers will routinely be reviewed by organisational supervisors and the courts in each specific case. However, the low visibility of routine policing decisions, on the streets or in the station, makes it difficult to assess the propriety of actions where there are contested versions of what happened.

c. House-keeping Decisions

Decisions about internal organisational matters may be couched in mandatory form and sanctioned effectively if they are not implemented. The controversial issues here arise from the impossibility of demarcating such decisions from law enforcement. Organisational changes inevitably have *some* effect on operations. Thus when for example during the 1984-85 miners' strike South Yorkshire Police Authority sought to disband the Mounted Division on the house-keeping grounds that the strike imposed too much of a burden on police resources, the force responded successfully by attacking this as a back-door attempt to influence controversial operations.

d. Personnel Management

The other kind of internal organisational matter concerns specific decisions about managing individual officers: should particular officers be selected for particular posts, promoted, discipline, redeployed? As with general organisational policy questions, career decisions about specific officers have implications for law enforcement. The character of the officers recruited in a force, deployed to particular duties or postings, and promoted to command level structures the pattern of law enforcement decisions in the force as a whole.

Conclusion

The types of decision made by police vary according to a number of factors making them easier or harder to review. Internal organisational decisions, whether they concern individual cases or general policies are made explicitly and with formal records which constitute the decision. They are thus readily reviewable in principle, if it is agreed that they should be made accountable to outside bodies.

Decisions concerning law enforcement relate to events which occur outside the organisation's direct control. If they concern general policies then they are explicitly formulated and hence reviewable in principle. However, as long as the notion of constabulary independence holds sway they will be couched in permissive or exhortatory rather than mandatory form. They will be statements of intent which may ultimately have little impact on the officers carrying out operations on the ground, rather than specific, sanctioned instructions to use legal powers in specified ways in particular situations. The doctrine of constabulary independence preserves a considerable degree of discretion for police officers about how they use their legal powers in specific cases. When they are used, the outcome results in some formal record, and if prosecution follows the case will be reviewed by a variety of other actors in the criminal justice process. Decisions *not* to invoke legal powers in particular cases are much harder to review, and normally will not be.

If disputes arise about how constables exercise their legal powers
these are particularly problematic to investigate and adjudicate. Most
encounters between police and suspects are low visibility ones, with
no independent witnesses, and suspects are often low in the
hierarchy of social credibility. Their word is unlikely to prevail
against a police officer's in the absence of independent
corroboration of some sort. The paradoxical consequence is that the
most crucial decisions about policing are made case-by case by the
lowest ranks in the organisation. They accumulate into working
policies which are not explicitly formulated and almost intractable
to review. On the other hand, the formal organisational policies
which are couched as such have an uncertain and indirect impact on
the real pattern of law enforcement on the streets.

To Whom Should the Police be Accountable?

Police officers are accountable to internal supervisory officers for
their conduct with respect to the rules of law and the police
disciplinary code. Their efficiency is also monitored by internal
management processes. This is itself uncontroversial in principle.
What raises acute argument and debate is the questions of what
external agencies police officers should also be accountable to.

It is uncontentious that police officers are accountable to the law in
the concrete shape of the courts. This is in a double-sense. They
may be tried for misconduct amounting to a criminal offence, or
sued for damages if it is alleged that they committed a tort against
a member of the public. In addition, the propriety of their conduct
will also be assessed by the courts in relation to the criminal cases
they have constructed. If it is held that they have gathered evidence
in violation of proper procedures, for example those specified under
the Police and Criminal Evidence Act 1984 (PACE) it may be that
such evidence is excluded. Even if it is not, internal disciplinary
proceedings may be initiated. Since the Prosecution of Offence Act
1985, which established the Crown Prosecution Service, police
decisions to prosecute are also subject to the scrutiny of formally
independent lawyers before a prosecution is launched. This is
intended to be a check not only on impropriety but police

craftsmanship and policy in constructing cases for the prosecution, although its effectiveness is debatable. (McConville, Sanders and Leng 1991).

The most controversial issues concern police accountability to independent external bodies which are not part of the legal process. There are two vexed areas. As indicated earlier, the machinery for handling complaints against individual police officers arising out of specific incidents remains one in which there is little public confidence, despite a variety of reform attempts since 1964. A wide body of opinion supports the idea that only a fully independent system for processing, investigating and adjudicating all complaints would ensure that justice is done and seen to be done.

The other thorny areas concern accountability for policy decisions as distinct from specific cases. The tripartite structure of governance derived from the 1964 Police Act is criticised from a number of points of view. There are basically two dimensions of debate about who the police should be accountable to for policy-making. (What type of accountability this should be will be considered in the next section). How should representatives of the public be selected? Should accountability be primarily local or national?

Selecting Representatives

At present the primary method of selecting representatives is the electoral process. The Home Secretary is a member of the elected government of the day. Two-thirds of local police authority members are elected councillors. This has been attacked from two contrasting viewpoints. Police opinion has often criticised police authority members for being either unrepresentative or lacking adequate expertise or both (cf. Reiner 1991, Chap. 11). Police officers have often argued for a form of appointment rather than election of local representatives to counter this. (Anderton 1981; Oliver 1987). Local police authorities should, it is argued, be selected so as to be representative of those interests with a legitimate stake in policing decisions, for example, professional, residents' and business associations. Kenneth Clarke's proposals announced on 23 March 1993 would replace the current control of local police authorities by elected members, in favour of central government appointees. He claimed this would make them more 'powerful and businesslike'.

On the other hand there has been strong support for the opposite view that local representatives should be chosen entirely by the electoral process and that the one-third JP element is anomalous. This has long been the view of Labour and the Liberal Democrats and was supported by the Widdicombe Committee in 1986[3]. The same body of opinion supports the idea of an elected local police authority in London, ending the anomalous position whereby the Metropolitan Police uniquely lack a local police authority. This view is now supported also by a majority of chief constables themselves (Reiner 1991, pp. 263-4). Although the government has now accepted the legitimacy of a local police authority for the metropolis, this is in a context of increasing central government control over *all* police authorities, and will not give the local electorate the dominant voice.

Apart from the issue of whether police authorities should consist of elected or appointed members, there is the vexed issue of the balance between local and national governance. Although originally created on a local basis in the 19th century, British police forces have become more and more centrally regulated and standardised during this century. The Royal Commission on the Police 1960-2 did consider whether or not to change the organisation of policing to a national force. Despite a cogent dissenting memorandum from Professor Goodhart, the majority report settled on the compromise which was adopted by the 1964 Police Act. Locally organised forces would remain but with the Home Secretary acquiring more responsibilities and powers. The continuing centralising trend since then was consolidated by the 1985 Local Government Act which considerably enhanced central financial control. It was reflected in the landmark decision in the Northumbria Police Authority case in 1988[4]. In this judgement the Court of Appeal held that, in a dispute over what type of spending was required for effective policing, the views of the Home Secretary would prevail over local police authorities, both as a correct interpretation of their respective roles under the Police Act 1964 and by virtue of the Royal Prerogative to maintain the peace.

Whilst the centralising trend is clear, debate still flourishes about how to react to it. Should it be accepted as inevitable, perhaps even desirable, and attention concentrated on constructing adequate national accountability mechanisms for policing? Or should attempts be made to reverse the process, by beefing-up local police authorities and bringing a greater measure of equality to the tripartite system?

In recent years the debate about the locus of police accountability has been extended beyond this perennial local/national argument. As British police have become involved increasingly in associations with police in other countries, in particular with the advent of the single market in Europe, so concern has developed about how the growing phenomenon of multi-national police co-operation can be made accountable.

Whilst debate has raged about what bodies the police should be accountable to and how they should be constituted, it is difficult to see any argument in principle from exempting the police from ultimate control by elected governmental institutions, as is true of all other public services. In a democracy, basic questions of what values should be embodied in policies and with what priority they should be pursued, are in the final analysis to be decided by the electoral process. Arguments against this have tended to *ad hominem* ones, against particular politicians as inappropriate people for deciding on police matters. Alternatively they have rested upon a technocratic notion that policing decisions should be decided by professional experts. Mr Clarke's stated rationale for his current proposals - to make the police more 'businesslike' - epitomises this technocratic fallacy. Although decisions ought to be informed by expertise and experience, the ends to which policy is directed is a political not a technical question, which should be determined by the electorate, not 'experts'. This, however, leaves open important questions about how best to arrange institutions to achieve police accountability.

What Type of Police Accountability?

Some years ago Geoffrey Marshall developed an important distinction between two types of accountability. He called them the 'subordinate and obedient' and the 'explanatory and co-operative' styles (Marshall 1978, pp. 61-3).

The 'explanatory and co-operative' style is the conception of accountability which underlies the Police Act 1964. Chief constables have obligations to provide police authorities with an annual report, as well as further reports which the authority may ask for on any matter connected with the policing of an area (s.12). Such reports may be refused if the chief constable deems this to be in the public interest, or believes the report not to be 'needed for the discharge of the functions of the police authority'. In the event of such disagreement, the Home Secretary arbitrates. The police authority does appoint, and may dismiss 'in the interest of efficiency', the chief constable (as well as deputy and assistant chief constables). However, these powers are subject to the Home Secretary's approval.

In essence, chief constables have a duty to present police authorities with accounts of their policies but are not *bound* to take any notice of the views of the authority. The majority of chief constables do take great pains to cultivate harmonious relationships with their police authorities, but this is a matter of wise statecraft rather than bowing to the powers of police authorities (Reiner 1991, Chap. 11). For their part, police authorities have normally accepted the claims to professional expertise of chief officers and been content to follow their guidance. When in the early and mid 1980s the radical Labour police authorities in the metropolitan areas sought to exert more control over policing policy they were consistently defeated. Eventually they were abolished by the Local Government Act 1985 and replaced by the generally more pliable joint boards.

The Home Secretary does wield more formidable powers over chief constables and these powers (unlike the police authority's) are not subject to the arbitration of a third party (although they are

judicially reviewable for complete unreasonableness). The Home
Secretary can veto candidates for chief officer posts (and of course
directly appoints the Metropolitan Commissioner), can require police
authorities to call upon chief constables to retire and can require
reports from chief constables on any policing matters. Above all, he
or she exercises the most formidable power of the purse, with the 51
per cent direct central government contribution to local policing
costs (and the further revenue support grant element) being
dependent (at least in theory) upon HMIC certifying forces as
efficient. The criteria of efficiency are increasingly specified tightly
by the Home Office and spelled out in the ever growing number of
regulations and circulars it issues to forces on all aspects of policing
policy. Above all, the Home Office wields considerable influence on
the processes which shape the outlook of chief police officers, in
particular through its control of the central training institutions.
(Reiner 1991).

Whilst the Home Office does possess a formidable array of powers
by which it could control chief officers, its relationship with them
tends to be co-operative rather than confrontational. Its guidance as
expressed in circulars is normally the product of prior consultation
with the Association of Chief Police Officers (ACPO) and other
expressions of professional opinion, aimed at achieving a consensus
about appropriate policies.

The tripartite system thus works in the 'explanatory and co-
operative' style as its normal mode, even though the powers of local
police authorities are distinctly less than the other two parties and
arguably, if push came to shove, the Home Secretary is clearly the
dominant corner of the triangle. A strong line of critical opinion has,
however, argued since the 1964 Police Act that local police
authorities ought to have the ultimate power to determine policing
policies for their areas and that chief constables should be
'subordinate and obedient' to them. This was the original position
with most urban forces whose Watch Committees in the 19th
century did wield power over their chief officers. A line of academic
commentators has argued cogently that there is no valid reason for
treating policing policy as different from other public services, the

goals of which are determined ultimately by elected governments. If policing is regarded primarily as a local service then locally elected representative should be the dominant voice shaping policing in their areas. (Marshall 1965 - although he subsequently retracted from this position in his 1978 article; Jefferson and Grimshaw 1984; Lustgarten 1986). This viewpoint became dominant in Labour Party thinking in the late 1970s and early 1980s and it was party policy to restructure the 1964 Act so as to give local police authorities clear control over policy.

Until recently the accountability debate was between respective advocates of the 'explanatory and co-operative' vs. 'subordinate and obedient' modes. Mr. Clarke's proposals of 23 March 1993, coupled with leaked indications of what the Sheehy Report will recommend, suggest that a third mode is in the offing. This can be called 'calculative and contractual', and it parallels Conservative government policy in health, education and other public services. Local police authorities and chief constables are to be given complete freedom for the allocation of their budgets, the bulk of which will come from central government. However, they will be responsible in very strict ways for their stewardship of the budget. Police authorities will largely be accountable to central government through the mechanism of appointment. Chief police officers will be accountable primarily through a market mechanism. They will be appointed on short-term contracts and receive performance related pay (PRP). Their performance will be judged according to the achievement of a limited range of performance indicators. Mr. Clarke announced that these will include crime clear-up rates and response times to calls from the public. It is possible that Sheehy will also recommend short-term contracts and PRP for all police officers, and Mr Clarke announced new incapability procedures for officers not coming up to the mark.

The combined effect of these changes is a new mode of accountability, side-stepping without displacing the constabulary independence doctrine, Constables will remain formally free to exercise their powers according to their professional judgement in individual cases. They will be acutely aware, however, that their

total performance must reach the required targets or they will suffer
in the pocket and ultimately join the dole queues. This is likely to
be the over-riding factor in their decision-making. Behind a facade
of greater local autonomy over the allocation of budgets, the Home
Secretary will acquire an unprecedented degree of central control
over police decision-making, for s/he (together with central
government appointees) will determine the criteria for performance
and assess their attainments. Small wonder the editor of *Police
Review* recently declared this amounted to the basis for a police
state in Britain (Hilliard and Pead 1993). Police officers will be
constrained to consider only a limited number of *ends* of policing,
and be encouraged implicitly to be less concerned about the legality
of the tactic used to achieve them or the impact on the quality of
police public relations. A decade of post-Scarman reforms will be
sabotaged.

What Mechanisms can Achieve Accountability?

The principles of police accountability - For What? To Whom? How
Much? - are deeply contested. Whatever the concept of
accountability that is pursued, however, there are further problems
of how to construct concrete mechanisms that will achieve its
substance rather than merely the formal trappings. Explanatory
accountability lacks teeth and runs the danger of degenerating into
an empty charade or manipulated consensus. The converse danger
with the 'humble and obedient' style is that it may be vitiated by the
problem of the inevitable discretion constables exercise in their
routine operations, protected by the low visibility of most police
work. The 'calculative and contractual' mode preferred by Mr
Clarke *does* penetrate the reality of police decisions, but is
concerned only with a limited range of outcomes. This neglects any
consideration of the legitimacy of the process by which results are
achieved or the quality of relations with the public.

The noted Policy Studies Institute study of policing in London
suggested an important distinction between three types of rule which
relate to police practices (Smith *et al* 1983, Vol. IV pp.169-72).
'Presentation rules' were ones which put an acceptable gloss on

police behaviour, but bore little relation to those which actually governed them. 'Inhibitory rules' were those which were formulated tightly, and were subject to effective sanctions. These exercised a deterrent effect on police conduct whether or not they reached their hearts and minds. 'Working rules' were those which police officers had internalised as part of their informal culture and actually guided their behaviour in the absence of any effective inhibitory mechanisms.

The task of building adequate institutions of police accountability must avoid constructing merely presentational rules. The problem in relying on inhibitory rules solely is that the low visibility, high discretion nature of police work makes it hard to have rules which can be enforced with sufficient consistency to become effective deterrents, apart from highly specific situations like booking-in procedures (which take place in open areas in police stations to which supervisors have regular access). The market mechanism emphasises the quantity of specific outputs at the expense of the *quality* of police practice. Ideally the aim must be to influence the 'working rules' of police culture, by changing the socialisation process and the organisational rewards in appropriate ways, backed up by 'inhibitory rules' but not depending on them. A project which seeks like this one to offer recommendations for achieving police accountability must bear in mind the warning words of a distinguished American scholar:

'... The art of achieving accountability.. is to enlist the support of the police in disciplinary activities... For processes of external regulation.. to be more than a highly publicised morality play, the police must become convinced that they will be trusted to bear the active responsibility for ensuring correct performance.' (Bayley, 1983, p.158).

Effective accountability means winning the hearts and minds of the police themselves for the values of democratic policing, not just securing token compliance and mute insubordination.

Notes

1. cf. *R v. Chief Constable of the Devon and Cornwall Constabulary, ex.p. CEGB* [1981] 3 All ER 826.

2. eg. *R. v Oxford, ex.p. Levey, The Times* 1 November 1986.

3. *The Conduct of Local Authority Business* Cmnd. 9797.

4. *R v Secretary of State for the Home Department, ex.p. Northumbria Police Authority* [1988] 2 WLR 590.

Bibliography

Anderton J (1981) 'The Art and Economics of Policing' Paper presented to SSRC Public Policy Study Group Seminar on Central and Local Government Relations. London: Royal Institute of Public Administration.

Bayley D (1983) 'Accountability and Control of Police : Some Lessons for Britain'. In Bennett T (ed) *The Future of Policing* (Cropwood Papers 15) Cambridge: Institute of Criminology.

Grimshaw R and Jefferson T (1987) *Interpreting Policework* London: Unwin.

Hilliard B and Pead D (1993) 'Are we heading for a police state?' *Police Review* 14 May.

Jefferson T and Grimshaw R (1984) *Controlling the Constable* London: Muller.

Loveday B (1991) 'The New Police Authorities' *Policing and Society* 1:3.

Lustgarten L (1986) *The Governance of the Police* London: Sweet and Maxwell.

Maguire M and Corbett C (1991) *A study of the Police Complaints System* London: HMSO.

Marshall G (1965) *Police and Government* London: Methuen.

Marshall G (1978) 'Police Accountability Revisited' in Butler D and Halsey A (eds) *Policy and Politics* London: Macmillan.

McConville M, Sanders A and Leng R (1991) *The Case for the Prosecution* London: Routledge.

Morgan R and Smith D (eds) *Coming To Terms With Policing* London: Routledge.

Reiner R (1991) *Chief Constables* Oxford: Oxford University Press.

Reiner R (1992) *The Politics Of The Police* 2nd. ed. Hemel Hempstead: Wheatsheaf.

Smith D, Gray J and Small S (1983) *Police And People In London* London: Police Studies Institute.

2. MEASURING POLICE PERFORMANCE: ACCOUNTING OR ACCOUNTABILITY?
Mollie Weatheritt

Since the late 1970s, the police force has moved from being a largely closed institution to one that has become more open to outside scrutiny and more receptive to the need for critical evaluation. Part of this development has involved a greater emphasis than before on the importance of developing accessible and explicit definitions about what is to count as performance. This paper sets out to trace the career of an ambiguous, shifting and negotiable concept - police performance - from its roots in concerns about how to improve the managerial accountability of the police to a more recent, and still evolving, interest in how performance information might be used to generate first, improved political accountability and second, greater responsiveness to those who use or otherwise benefit from police services.

The issues raised by performance measurement are both technical and political. In many public services, perhaps particularly in the police service, the technical problems involved in measuring performance are daunting. The relationships between inputs, outputs and outcomes - between the assignment of resources, what gets done and what effects that activity has - are not infrequently complex, tenuous, unknown and difficult to know. The goals of policing are multiple and may conflict; the attainment of goals for which the service is routinely held accountable (for example, public tranquillity or the absence of crime) may only partially, minimally, and to an unknown extent be dependent on police action; and the outputs of policing are often intangible and not readily identifiable. It is not the purpose of this paper to dwell upon or to explore in detail these technical difficulties. While technical considerations will clearly have an important bearing on what is measured and how, these choices raise more fundamental questions of how the police should be judged, by whom and for what purposes. What is measured, which institutions measure it and how they then use and make available to others the results of such measurement provide an important barometer of official thinking on police accountability more generally. It is on these political and institutional issues that I propose to focus in this paper.

The thinking about police performance has tended to be driven by the concerns of central government both as guardian of the public purse and as probably *the* key influence, deriving from its *de facto* status within the tripartite structure of police governance, on the development of policing policy. However, since the late 1980s, the police force itself has contributed more openly and more effectively to discussions about the purposes of policing and to the development of appropriate evaluative criteria. Police authorities, by contrast, have been largely (although not entirely) silent, an unfortunate reflection both of their status within the tripartite structure and of the way in which they have chosen to discharge their statutory duty to provide adequate and efficient forces. An increasingly important institutional player, which is independent of government and also stands outside the tripartite structure, has been the Audit Commission. The Commission has raised some uncomfortable questions about the adequacy both of performance measures *per se* and of systems of performance review. It has also emerged as a champion of police authorities. Additionally, these different institutional players, of differing power and influence, have been joined in recent years by 'customers' - members of the public whose views about the kinds of policing they want are increasingly being sought and who are seen as an important potential audience for performance information on the police.

Home Office Circular 114/1983

The root of current preoccupations with measuring police performance lies in the wish of successive Conservative governments to introduce value for money disciplines - economy, efficiency and effectiveness (joined subsequently by excellence and enterprise) - into the management of public services. Since the early 1980s, government departments have been required to have 'a clear view of their objectives and means to assess and, wherever possible, measure outputs or performance in relation to those objectives'

(HMSO, 1982). In 1983, the Home Office signalled what this meant for the police service in a key circular, *Manpower, efficiency and effectiveness in the police service* (Home Office 1983). This enjoined chief officers and police authorities to formulate clear objectives and priorities for their force; and to do so in ways which were both 'best calculated to reflect the wishes and needs of the public' and took into account the views and experience of junior officers.

Forces were asked to consider putting in place systems which would enable them to assess whether objectives had been achieved and, in a subsequent circular, increases in force establishments were made conditional on forces being able to demonstrate, 'where possible [by] quantified output and performance measures', that objectives were being met (Home Office, 1988). Circular 114 also spelled out a new, key role for Her Majesty's Inspectors of Constabulary in enhancing police effectiveness. HMICs were to be responsible for assessing how effectively chief officers, working with the police authority and local community, identified policing problems, set objectives, deployed resources and reviewed performance. In short, HMICs were to become arbiters of the effectiveness of not just the managerial but also the political processes involved in performance review.

I have described circular 114/1983 as a key one, but what of its effects? The circular marked the beginning of what has become a persistent and high-profile pursuit of better value for money in police forces. It has undoubtedly helped to generate a much more performance conscious culture within forces and laid the foundation for much subsequent work, such that the Audit Commission has concluded that 'a great deal of effort' now goes into performance measurement (Audit Commission, 1990a). More specifically it led to a flurry of force mission statements - broad statements of what a force is trying to achieve - which all police forces now produce as a matter of course. In addition, virtually all forces have made efforts to put in place the management systems (most of them variants of policing by objectives) for linking that mission statement to the production of more specific local objectives aimed at generating purposeful, planned activity by junior operational officers and at measuring the results of that activity[1].

On the face of it, pbo has been enthusiastically adopted by forces. A study in which I have been involved has found that between 20 and 30 local objectives are produced annually by police sub-divisions, that is, approximately one per fortnight. Virtually all operational officers are aware of and do work in relation to at least some of those objectives. However, the way in which objectives are formulated and reviewed leaves much to be desired, both managerially and in terms of the requirements of public accountability.

The managerial difficulties with pbo can be simply stated. Objectives are often formulated on the basis of poor, irrelevant or incomplete information; in other words on the basis of an inadequate definition of what the problem is. They are often unrealistic, particularly when they seek reductions in crime; at a formal level at least, officers seem reluctant to specify the limits to police action and effectiveness. Officers feel they have inadequate time in which to work on objectives. Evaluation is, more often than not, inadequate, either because relevant information is not readily available, or because available information is misused, leading to what one chief superintendent has memorably described as police action inevitably being 'doomed to success'. There is little evidence that pbo has been used to identify, consolidate and build upon successful performance and to review and learn from less successful performance. Organisationally, the results of objective-related activity tend to lead nowhere; the expectation that pbo would provide the basis for laying bare and spreading good practice seems not have been fulfilled.

The extent to which the opportunities offered by pbo have served the interest of greater public accountability is unclear. Most chief officers and many sub-divisional commanders would claim to involve local consultative groups in the process of setting local policing objectives and it would, I guess, be an unusual local commander who was unaware of what the concerns of his or her local group were. It is clear too that certain local policing priorities are highly susceptible to public pressure, issues of rowdyism and public nuisance being prominent examples. But whether the kind of informational feedback to consultative groups on the nature and effectiveness of police action is anything more than ritualistic seems doubtful. The quality of information could, in any case, hardly be better than that which is collected for internal management purposes and, as I have argued, that quality is patchy. Yet despite the deficiencies in the information they collect for themselves, the police nonetheless are at a huge informational advantage over consultative groups, most of which do not have the resources with which to create a relevant and independently verifiable information base of their own or to question that of the police. Improved accountability at this level inevitably means better information: the creation both of an analytical capacity and a shared framework to guide its use.

At force (rather than sub-divisional) level, Circular 114 sees objective setting as a shared process, involving a partnership of equals - the chief constable and the police authority. It is doubtful whether this equality has anywhere been achieved; the Association of Metropolitan Authorities, for example, has stated that the formulation of objectives has been done by chief constables, with the police authority having less influence than (unrepresentative) consultative groups and limited to giving retrospective agreement to the chief constable's proposals (AMA 1991). In other words, the informational, political and professional advantages have all lain with the force. Police authorities can do little about the last of these; they may feel inhibited from exercising a greater political authority (the AMA survey found that the level of advice and guidance that police authorities offered to chief constables was both very low and highly parochial); but they can do a great deal about the first. Like consultative groups, however, whom they are responsible for resourcing, police authorities seem to have paid little attention to developing an analytical capacity of their own. While this no doubt reflects their junior partner status within the tripartite structure, it also tends to reinforce it. While greater local political accountability may yet depend on a recasting of the respective responsibilities of chief officer, police authorities and the Secretary of State set out in the Police Act 1964, there is thus much that police authorities can do to strengthen their hand within the present arrangements. Circular 114 provided a wedge in the door, if such were needed. Later initiatives, discussed below, take this process further.

HM Inspectorate of Constabulary

The Inspectorate has traditionally been the least politically and organisationally visible part of the tripartite structure although, as we shall see, that status is changing. HMIs have a statutory duty under the Police Act 1964 to 'inspect and report to the Secretary of State on the efficiency of all the police forces': the exchequer grant to the police authority, amounting to 51 per cent of police expenditure, is conditional upon the force receiving a certificate of efficiency from the HMIC. HMIs are also required to 'carry out such other duties for furthering police efficiency as the Secretary of State may from time to time direct'. They are, for example, an important means by which the policy concerns of the Home Office are conveyed to and impressed upon the police service. They are a conduit for conveying police service views back to government and a means by which the Home Office gains information on how its policy priorities are being implemented in the field. They also have a key role in identifying good policing practice and disseminating it more widely.

The format and content of inspections have never been statutorily defined although they have become increasingly administratively regulated as part of the Home Office response to the financial management initiative. In 1983, the Inspectorate was asked to work to more explicit guidelines than had hitherto been available in determining force efficiency and in probing force performance. This guidance is set out annually in a series of policy statements and a set of questions to which forces are asked to provide answers prior to each inspection round. The 1993 guidance comprises over 40 policy statements and about 300 questions in relation to seven key areas: personnel and organisation; use of technology; 'operational performance' - mainly crime information; quality of service;

community relations; complaints and discipline; counter-terrorism
and war emergency planning. In essence, three different sorts of
information are required from forces: descriptions of what is
happening backed where appropriate by numerical data; information
on the monitoring and assessment systems that the force has in
place; and evaluative information on whether policies are working
and how performance has improved.

In the area of performance review, where the policy is 'to encourage
forces to establish an independent system of internal inspection',
forces are thus asked to describe existing inspection procedures and
what performance indicators are used to assess force performance,
and to assess what improvements have been achieved as a result of
inspection and performance review. Under community relations,
forces are asked what role consultative groups have in agreeing and
monitoring local standards of service, what steps the force is taking
to overcome any difficulties they might have in maintaining
effective liaison with ethnic minority groups and what improvements
in quality of service have resulted from public consultation
exercises. The Inspectorate is given no guidance, nor has it
developed any for itself, on how to go about answering these
questions, so that the process of inspection remains largely one of
gaining the kind of professional feel for the force that is born of
considerable police experience. (All HMIs are ex chief officers and
their support staffs, who undertake most of the work preparatory to
formal inspection, are almost all serving police officers.)

That said, professional feel has come to be supported by an
increasing quantity of numerical data which the Inspectorate uses to
draw comparisons between forces (and between different operating
units within the same force) on, for example, the proportion of
female officers employed or the proportion of crimes detected by
various means. Such comparisons are mainly used to inform the
inspection process, to help inspectors probe behind and explore
possible reasons for deviations from the norm, and are not used
directly to inform public debate. The data set on which they are
based is known as the 'matrix of indicators' - around 700 items of
information in the areas of crime detection, manpower, community

relations and crime prevention, public order, traffic and criminal proceedings. Since the mid 1980s, this data set has been added to, reclassified and computerised. This developmental process is still continuing and more thought seems likely to be given to exploiting more fully its analytical potential, both as a research resource for inspectors and as a basis for generating comparative key performance indicators (see further below).

Inspectorate reports on forces have been published since 1990 when the then Home Secretary announced a return to a tradition of reporting publicly on individual forces which dated from the establishment of the Inspectorate in the mid-nineteenth century but which had long since lapsed. One aim of publication was to increase public awareness of what the Inspectorate does. Another was to bring evidence of deficiencies in force performance into the public domain and by so doing generate increased pressure for improvement. In 1991, further innovations were announced. HMIs would carry out inspection over the full range of force responsibilities - that is, the seven key areas referred to above - only once every two years, while an intermediate inspection, covering a limited number of topics but in greater depth, would be published in the intervening years. (Community relations and quality of service have been popular candidates for intermediate inspections.) In addition there was to be a greater concentration on 'thematic' inspections, the examination of specific topic areas across a range of forces.

Since the Home Secretary's initial announcement, the Inspectorate has published well over 100 reports on individual forces. From them we can begin to see how the Inspectorate judges the performance of forces and what policies it (and the Home Office) wish to see pursued. There are few surprises. The reports cover civilianisation, equal opportunities policies, information technology strategy, management style, quality of service issues, patterns of crime and so on. The reports are by no means complacent. They are invariably critical of aspects of force practice and from time to time are likely to make uncomfortable reading for police authorities, whose funding policies and/or commitment to more effective community liaison arrangements are apt to provoke adverse inspectorial comment. That said, however, their factual emphasis and their bureaucratic and coded prose seem far from calculated to promote greater public awareness of what the Inspectorate does, let alone stimulate greater local debate of the important policing issues that the reports cover[2].

Moreover, save in relation to a limited number of areas (for example, the proportion of women police officers and their representation in specialist posts), reports under-exploit the rich comparative database afforded by the matrix of indicators. Relatively low priority seems to have been given to thematic inspections, areas of practice where the intention was to highlight developments in a number of forces and begin to draw out implications for good practice; in other words to develop and exploit the Inspectorate's consultancy role. In short, while the publication of inspection reports has been a welcome innovation, its value lies as much in the implications it has for the effectiveness and evolution of the Inspectorate as for the effectiveness and evolution of police forces. In particular, more thought needs to be given to defining who the audiences for inspection material are and to promoting more effective ways of engaging with them; and to making more explicit the conceptual structure and the benchmarks that inspectors use in reaching their judgements.

The Audit Commission

The future form and content and, indeed, precise purposes of inspection have been made more relevant and pressing by the entry of the Audit Commission onto the policing scene. The Commission was created by the Local Government Finance Act 1982 to extend the financial audit function of its predecessor, the District Audit Service, by monitoring and promoting economy, efficiency and effectiveness in the management of local government. (The Commission's remit was later extended to cover the NHS under the NHS and Community Care Act 1990.) Its two main duties are to appoint auditors to local authorities and NHS bodies and to undertake studies to promote economy, efficiency and effectiveness. Auditors have a broader brief than solely to ensure financial propriety; they are required to satisfy themselves that the authority is making economic, efficient and effective use of resources. In order that they may discharge this latter duty effectively, the Commission supplies auditors with material based on its special study work. These audit guides set out performance standards where appropriate and provide auditors with a methodology for their work (Audit Commission,1991a; the undated Audit Guides are listed in the bibliography to this paper). The Commission is independent of government. Indeed, it is under a statutory duty to undertake studies of the effect on local government economy, efficiency and effectiveness of ministerial directions and guidance.

In 1988, the Commission published the first of what is now a series of eleven special studies on the police. Although in the decade up to 1988 the police service had become increasingly accustomed to scrutiny by informed professional outsiders, most notably through the growth of independent police research, the Commission's independent professional authority, its specialist expertise and its legal status and powers have clearly been a source of threat (potential if not actual) to a service where overall performance review has typically been self-generated (internal management) or carried out by professional peers (the Inspectorate). The Commission's work programme and the way in which that programme has developed demonstrates a political astuteness born of the need to win the confidence, from a standing start, of those within its police constituency whom it seeks to influence. It thus began with reviews of subject areas where it had gained experience from its other local government work and where it might be presumed to stand on uncontroversial ground - those administrative and other services which seek to support rather than drive police operational practice and which are normally provided by civilian staff (Audit Commission 1988a and b; 1989).

The Audit Commission's recent studies (Audit Commission 1990a, 1991b & c) trespass more openly on the kinds of professional and managerial territory from which, ironically enough given district auditors' newly-created remit in these areas, police authorities have either been excluded (whether deliberately or by default) or have voluntarily absented themselves. They include systems of performance review, ways of allocating resources, local financial management and management (territorial command) structures. (The Commission's current study of the operational heartland represented by the CID, represents an even bolder move.) The Commission is well aware of the sensitivities likely to be involved by auditors' entry into this territory; indeed, the introduction to the relevant audit guide carries an explicit warning to this effect[3].

Like the Inspectorate of Constabulary, the Audit Commission has a statutory policing role which, again like the Inspectorate, it has increasingly combined with a consultancy stance. Like the Inspectorate, its influence depends largely on its capacity to persuade; to act in such a way as to promote a professional, managerial and political consensus about emergent good practice and what is to count as good performance. While the knowledge base from which inspectors seek to influence the police service has been a largely unspoken one, however, and draws its authority from HMICs' status as senior fellow professionals, the Commission's powers of persuasion have depended on the creation of a more explicit empirical (and hence in the current climate more secure) knowledge base. Commission reports, unlike those of Inspectors, have been conceived primarily as a vehicle for argument, backed up by description and analysis. They are stylish, well written and attention grabbing and have a direction and cohesion which, although not lacking from inspection reports, are far more apparent.

This direction and cohesion owes much to a clear and explicit view of what characterises a good local authority (and, by implication, a good police service). Derived from Peters' and Waterman's characterisation, in *In search of excellence*, of the successful private sector concern, it is one which: understands its customers; responds to the electorate; sets and pursues clear and consistent objectives; assigns clear management responsibilities; trains and motivates people; communicates effectively; monitors results; and adapts quickly to change (Audit Commission 1988c). This prescriptivism inevitably finds its way into the audit guides which, unlike inspection guidance notes, set out a detailed methodology for approaching particular issues. (The audit guide on performance review for example, asks auditors to discuss with constables, sergeants and inspectors how well aims and objectives are communicated within the force, whether junior officers are aware of them and whether they influence officers' behaviour. While HMIs may indeed do precisely this, they are not specifically enjoined to.) Unlike inspection reports, auditors' detailed reports are not published, being the property of the local authority concerned, although their main conclusions are.

While most of the Commission's value for money work on the police service has inevitably been addressed to internal management issues, it has also been at pains to help develop a less supine and more constructive role for police authorities in line with its view that democratic responsiveness is one of the preconditions for effective performance. In its special study on police finance (Audit Commission 1990b) the Commission argued that the way in which central government uses its powers to control major capital expenditure and the numbers of police officers has eroded not just the provisioning responsibilities of police authorities but also any incentives they might have had to promote better police performance; the more power that central government has accreted to itself, the less interested and effective have police authorities become in developing their own role. While restoring these incentives (and creating new ones) will ultimately require changes in the way in which central government finances the police, the Commission believes that there nonetheless remains scope for police authorities to develop their role within existing arrangements.

The basis for this development is to be the production of output-based quantifiable performance indicators based on specified standards of service delivery which police authorities should be to the fore in formulating (Audit Commission 1990a). In drawing up such standards, police authorities should adopt the role of 'champion of the consumers', identifying local needs by undertaking public surveys and by promoting the development of local consultative groups as 'representative' consumer fora (Flannery, 1992)[4]. Police authorities should, moreover, adopt a higher profile in representing

forces to local communities, taking on more responsibility in public
debate about standards and ensuring that quality issues remain on
the policing agenda.

As we shall see, at least some of these proposals raise as many
questions as they answer and fulfilling such a brief is unlikely to
prove particularly easy for many police authorities (nor, given their
current role, particularly attractive for some). They have, however,
been helped to the starting gate by the Commission's duty, under
the Local Government Act 1992, to specify lists of indicators of
performance on which every local authority will be obliged to report
annually. The Commission has set out 20 such indicators for the
police (Audit Commission, undated), covering the five key
operational areas outlined by the Association of Chief Police
Officers as a result of its own work on quality issues (the indicators
are also listed at the end of this chapter). It is this work, and related
developments within central government, to which I now turn.

Quality of service

The police have not been content to remain just as the recipients of
much fine advice about the importance of performance review, they
have also been busy themselves. At the end of 1990, the Association
of Chief Police Officers launched a statement of corporate values,
to which every force has subsequently signed up, which committed
the police force to improving the quality of police services in
partnership with the public (Association of Chief Police Officers,
1990). What precipitated this development was evidence, impossible
to gainsay, that public confidence in the police service was waning.
The British Crime Survey, published earlier in the year had shown
a 'steady erosion' in support for the police since the early 1980s.
Moreover, 'the nearer people's problems lay to the traditional core
of the police function, the more dissatisfied they were', (Skogan,
1990). The survey identified a gap, probably growing, between
people's expectations about the capacity of the police and their
ability to deliver services. The police already knew this for
themselves. The *Operational Policing Review*, researched by the
service itself, had identified not only dissatisfaction with and falling

confidence in police services, but also a gap between what professional (police) and lay (public) opinion felt should count as good performance (Joint Consultative Committee 1990). The service was concerned that, if it failed to take a lead in doing something about these identified deficiencies, others would do it for them. The service wanted to restore its credibility and part of doing that was being seen to take the initiative.

Although published by ACPO, the statement of corporate values was the product of a working party in which the Police Federation and Superintendents' Association were also involved and was intended to commit all three associations. (It also included representatives from the Home Office but not, significantly, local authorities.) The working party recommended that each force draw up a clear policy statement re-emphasising the responsibility of each member of the force to provide a fair, courteous and non-discriminatory service; identifying a management strategy and management responsibilities for carrying the policy through; identifying relevant performance indicators; and re-emphasising the 'central importance' of consulting the public. Reconstituted as a sub-committee of ACPO, the working party has continued to sit, its membership now including the local authority associations and representatives of police training establishments. It sees itself as 'the central focus for taking [the quality of service] initiative forward and in advising and supporting the work of individual forces'[5].

The working group has identified five 'key service areas' of policing which have provided the framework within which, with the addition of a category relating to the costs of policing, ACPO, the Audit Commission, the Inspectorate and the Home Office have subsequently sought to develop the key indicators of police performance most relevant to their respective constitutional and organisational priorities. Those key areas are the way in which forces handle calls from the public; crime management (for example crime reduction, victim support and crime investigation); traffic management; public reassurance and order maintenance; and community policing (Quality of Service Sub-Committee, 1991).

While the police service has understandably been keen to take the lead in developing indicators of 'quality', they were quickly joined by other institutional players. One result of this was that forces found themselves expected to generate an avalanche of information with no very clear rationale and uninformed by any clear statement of priorities. By the time the Audit Commission issued its consultation paper, ACPO itself had suggested that forces set (an unspecified but large number of) service delivery standards in relation to no less than 28 'core functions' (Quality of Service Sub-Committee, op cit), while the Inspectorate had indicated its intention to add to the matrix of indicators a further 45 relating specifically to service quality in order 'to identify how far forces have responded to meeting the requirements of [the ACPO Strategic Policy Document.]' (Inspectorate of Constabulary 1991). A more corporate approach to the development of key indicators was therefore thought to be needed. The results were announced in December 1992 (Quality of Service Sub-Committee, 1992). They comprise some three dozen indicators: the final list drawn up by the Audit Commission elaborated upon and added to by ACPO and the Inspectorate. (The complete list of indicators is shown in the Appendix to this chapter.)

A good performance indicator should deliver a clear message, be susceptible to management action and relevant to users' needs (Quality of Service Sub-Committee 1991; Audit Commission 1990a). The Audit Commission is committed, as part of the Citizen's Charter initiative, to developing published indicators that are 'relevant to citizens' - that are 'interesting and comprehensible'; which cover the amount of service provided, its effectiveness and quality, value for money and cost; and which support 'useful' comparisons, over time and between authorities (Audit Commission 1992). How far do the proposed packages of indicators themselves measure up to these criteria? *Which* citizens' values do they reflect and what sort of dialogue, in what fora and for what purposes is likely to be provoked by the publication of performance information? Will it create pressures towards improved performance and if so, how?

Performance, Consumerism and the Promotion of Active Citizenship

While the police service has, as part of its quality of service initiative, been keen to make policing more customer-friendly and to integrate questions about performance and service provision with the interests of *consumers*, the Audit Commission's concern that performance measures should reflect and promote the larger interests of *citizens* in theory go wider. In practice it is not easy to discern what conception of citizenship underlies the choice of indicators made by the Commission; nor is it easy conceptually to distinguish that choice from those made by the Inspectorate, and to a lesser extent ACPO, in drawing up their respective lists. Aside from the information it requires on workload and on resources and costs, the Commission's list requires local authorities to publish information relevant to issues of: equal opportunity in employment; accessibility and responsiveness (telephone answering and response times; time spent on patrol; the availability of female officers); effectiveness (detection rates, particularly in relation to the publicly salient crimes of burglary and violence); and consumer satisfaction (number of official complaints).

The Inspectorate too is concerned with issues of responsiveness (eg. in relation to the specific user interests represented by ethnic minorities it requires information on action taken in response to reports of racially motivated crime), and resource use. To these it adds measures of citizen involvement in participatory fora; and of the equity and acceptability of police action (cautioning rates and stop and search rates by ethnic group). ACPO's list concentrates solely on measures of public satisfaction with police services, particularly at points of access and mainly in non-adversarial contexts. Whilst this reflects a recognition that public concern about police performance derives from the nature of encounters, in proposing (and apparently taking control of) a national initiative in this regard, ACPO has clearly pipped police authorities to the post.

While much of the public service oriented literature on performance measurement is critical both of the narrow conception of consumer interests that such measurement often implies and of its top down nature (Pollitt 1988; Winkler 1987; Walsh 1991; Pfeffer and Coote 1991), such charges cannot be readily sustained in relation to the police. While they could hardly be said to dominate, issues of equity, fairness and citizen participation are by no means absent from a list of measures, part of which, at least, has been designed with public consumption in mind[6]. Moreover, the police service is well aware that its 'consumers' are not a homogeneous category with clearly defined common interests. That is implied by the intention, in collecting consumer opinion, to concentrate on particular categories and sub-groups of users: people calling the police; victims of crime in general and victims of racial incidents and domestic violence in particular; and people reported for traffic violations (although this last represents the only category with whom the police come into adversarial contact whose views about police action are to be sought).

Finally, those responsible for formulating the indicators have had the results of a great deal of user-oriented research on which to draw. This has enabled them to focus their measures on at least some user groups (for example victims) which are known to experience particular problems; and on issues (such as the number of bobbies on the beat) on which the public has consistently expressed a particular view. In addition, the Home Office has carried out small-group, consumer-based research which aims to assess whether the five key areas which form the framework into which performance information has been organised have relevance and salience for different groups. The Audit Commission has also announced its intention to carry out further research into issues which most concern citizens and into their opinions of the proposed measures.

A limited number of national performance indicators can do no more than represent a partial picture of police activities and performance. (An important omission is suspects - those enforced 'consumers' of police attention, on whom virtually no national performance indicators are being collected.) Moreover, no set of performance indicators, however apparently comprehensive, can offer a final judgement on the service to which they relate. Performance information, whether produced by or for auditors, inspectors, professionals, administrators or politicians is primarily a way of formulating and asking further questions and promoting a dialogue with service providers about the prospects for service improvement. That dialogue may well turn out to be no more then a sterile tussle over disputed meanings. It may fail to take place at all. In policing, the structures for encouraging and supporting such a dialogue at local level are not yet firmly in place; there has not been much evidence of serious local political interest in establishing them; and the nature of policing as a service to some extent militates against the establishment of such a dialogue.

I have already indicated that police authorities, on their present showing, may turn out to be diffident consumers of performance information, as well as junior (or even non-) partners in the business of setting local citizen's charter standards, the production of which the Audit Commission's indicators require. Several police forces have already published such standards (Kent, for example has been awarded the Chartermark for doing so). Unless police authorities begin to take the lead in discussions of standard setting they may find themselves relegated to the position in which they found themselves in relation to shared objective setting. The sampling of consumer opinion, for example, is already firmly in the hands of the police. Much of it is likely to remain so, if only because those forces that have set standards use routine customer sampling as a way of obtaining frequent feedback on performance. But the responsibility, for example, for surveying those people whose experiences and views are of interest and concern locally if not nationally, or groups whose interests are currently poorly reflected by the proposed ACPO-led surveys, could in theory pass to police authorities. It may be that HMICs should be invited to comment on the kinds of relationships established between chief officers and police authorities for promoting appropriate partnerships. There are precedents: HMICs already comment (not always favourably) on how police authorities discharge their statutory obligation to ensure

that the police can consult local communities on policing matters.
The AMA has said that it would welcome a closer advisory
relationship between police authorities and HMIC (Association of
Metropolitan Authorities 1991).

The (non adversarial) customers for policing differ from customers
of, for example, education and health care in that their contact with
the service tends to be intermittent, trivial and of short duration.
This limits the potential for developing the kinds of consumer
organisations and user groups that, in relation to other services, act
as solicitors and interpreters of performance information, as conduits
for it to the wider world and as a source of pressure on the service
concerned. The potential for developing this kind of active
citizenship in relation to policing is relatively limited but it is not
entirely absent. Neighbourhood watch associations, lay visitors
panels and victim support schemes each provide examples of groups
with a clear remit and an interest in a specific and relatively
constrained area of police performance where it might be possible
to develop local charter standards. Police authorities need to think
more systematically about how they might use information generated
by and for such groups as an additional approach to reflecting on
police performance. Lay visitors are an especially under-used
resource in this regard. They provide independent oversight of the
treatment of the most marginal and stigmatised of police 'customers'
- those in police custody - whose voice might otherwise go unheard.
(Lay visitors also, incidentally, provide free quality of service
inspections for police managers.) It is perhaps unfortunate that
relatively few police authorities have seen fit to nurture the growth
of such schemes.

It is inevitable that police/community consultative groups, despite
their unrepresentativeness, will increasingly come to be seen as
important fora for the articulation and, hopefully, incisive discussion
of police performance standards. Both the Home Office and the
Audit Commission have expressed a wish to see consultative groups
involved in this way and the development is a natural consequence
of the parallel move to devolve the responsibility for service
provision down to local command units with greater financial and

operational independence. Consultative groups moreover have a basis in statute, they are linked to their parent police authorities and their remit includes the gathering of local consumer opinion and consumer education. Their proposed involvement in charter issues - in the definition, setting and discussion of local standards of performance - may well serve as an antidote to what are, unfortunately, often little more than talking shops dominated by a police agenda (Morgan, 1989).

Conclusion

I have argued that the push towards better police performance measurement, while grounded in the wish to secure improved management accountability for the use of an expensive resource, has begun to move on to a different plane. Over the past few years there has been more emphasis on bringing a wider range of information than hitherto into the public domain with the express aim of promoting a more active public debate and, through it, increased pressures on service deliverers to improve their own performance. In particular there has been a conscious attempt to integrate questions about performance with the interests of consumers. One consequence of this is that it is no longer possible to make easy distinctions between the demands of management accountability and the requirement to account to external constituencies: similar performance information is relevant to the interests of each.

I have argued too that there have been persistent difficulties in creating vigorous and informed local oversight of and input into policing. While, as other chapters argue, tackling this issue will require a fundamental rethink of the role of local governance of the police, including a clearer specification of what police authorities themselves should be held accountable for, the requirement to publish nationally derived performance indicators for policing should of itself prompt greater police authority interest and involvement in local service delivery issues. First, even though the indicators have been imposed nationally, service standards have not. They are to be set locally and police authorities clearly have a role to play in doing so. Second, national performance indicators will only imperfectly reflect local priorities and concerns. A task for police authorities is the better to articulate these local concerns and to agree with the force relevant additional performance measures. Such agreements will inevitably involve decisions about what local policing priorities should be.

A commitment to developing a more robust and vigorous system of local consultation would help police authorities to gain a better purchase on what grass roots policing priorities are and would help create more effective local fora for holding the police to account. Consultative groups may themselves wish to agree with local police commanders performance measures relevant to local problems and concerns. If that is to happen, however, consultative groups will need to be adequately resourced (few police authorities spend more than a few thousand pounds per year on their consultative groups) and provided with relevant information and the capacity to analyse and reflect upon it.

Finally, a management postscript is perhaps in order. The task of improving police performance, that is, improving the standards of behaviour of individual police officers, can only be achieved if officers themselves come to believe that that is important and necessary. The police quality of service initiative involves imparting that sense of belief not just through obeisance to 'the customer' and what that implies for measures of police performance but also through the cultivation of a different organisational ethos and a different managerial style. In brief, nothing short of an internal cultural revolution has been proposed for policing - and by the police themselves. If performance measurement and the opportunities it brings to increase the external oversight of policing are to mean anything, it is important that they work with rather than against the grain of changes in management practice; that they be judged on the quality of debate they provoke *within* police forces, as well as that generated outside them.

Appendix: Performance indicators for the Police[7]

The following table shows the performance indicators for policing being required by the Audit Commission (AC) under the Local Government Act 1992; the Inspectorate of Constabulary (HMIC); and by ACPO - ACPO's indicators are, at this stage, advisory only.

Call Management

1.   HMIC   No. of incidents per 100 police officers.

2(a)   A.C.   No. of 999 calls received.

2(b)   A.C.   The local target for answering 999 calls.

2(c)   A.C.   The percentage of 999 calls answered within that target.

3(a)   A.C.   The local definition of 'incidents requiring immediate response'.

3(b)   A.C.   The number of such incidents.

3(c)   A.C.   The local target time(s) for responding to such incidents.

3(d)   A.C.   The percentage of responses to such incidents within the target time(s).

4   HMIC   Number of police vehicle accidents per police vehicle kilometre.

5   ACPO   Percentage of public satisfaction with police performance standards in relation to police action in response to 999 calls.

6   ACPO   Percentage of satisfaction of persons with service standard received at police station enquiry counters.

Crime Management

7(a) HMIC No. of PACE stop/searches of white persons per 1000 white population.

7(b) HMIC No. of PACE stop/searches of ethnic minority persons per 1000 ethnic minority population.

8(a) HMIC Percentage of files returned by CPS as unsatisfactory at first submission.

8(b) HMIC Percentage of files proceeded with by CPS.

8(c) HMIC Percentage of files sent to CPS which comply with time limits.

9(a) HMIC No. of persons arrested/reported for notifiable offences per 100 police officers.

9(b) HMIC Percentage of persons arrested/reported for notifiable offences prosecuted.

9(c) HMIC Percentage of persons arrested/reported for indictable offences cautioned.

9(d) HMIC Percentage of persons arrested/reported for notifiable offences dealt with by other means.

9(e) HMIC Percentage of persons arrested/reported for notifiable offences subject of no further action.

10   HMIC Percentage of reported racial incidents where further investigative action is taken.

11(a) A.C.   The number of recorded crimes:

     i. Total crime per 1000 population.
     ii. Violent crimes per 1000 population.

iii. Burglaries of dwellings per 1000 dwellings.

11(b) A.C. The percentage of crimes detected by primary and by other means (reported separately):

       i. All crimes.
      ii. Violent crime.
     iii. Burglaries of dwellings.

11(c) A.C. The number of crimes detected, by primary means, per officer.

12(a) ACPO Percentage of victims satisfied with police service standard at the time of initial response to report of violent crime.

12(b) ACPO Percentage of victims satisfied with police service standard at the time of initial response to report of burglary dwelling.

Traffic Management

13(a) HMIC Number of traffic offences per 100 police officers/traffic wardens.

13(b) HMIC Percentage of traffic offences dealt with by extended fixed penalty.

14(a) A.C. The number of screening breath tests administered.

14(b) A.C. The percentage of such breath tests which proved positive, or were refused by a driver.

15(a) A.C. The number of road traffic accidents involving death or personal injury.

15(b) A.C. The percentage of such accidents in which at least one driver tested positive for alcohol.

16   ACPO   Percentage of satisfaction of drivers with officer
              attitude when reported for a traffic violation.

17   ACPO   Percentage of satisfaction expressed by victims of
              road accidents with police service standard at the
              scene.

Public Order Management/Public Reassurance

18   HMIC   No. of Neighbourhood Watch Schemes per 1000
              households.

19   ACPO   Percentage of satisfaction of public with perceived
              levels of foot and mobile patrols.

20(a) ACPO   Percentage of satisfaction expressed by victims with
              police performance standards in relation to:

              a) racial incidents.

20(b) ACPO   b) domestic violence.

Community Policing Management

21   HMIC   Average attendance of persons attending meetings of
              consultative groups established under Section 106
              PACE Act 1984.

22   HMIC   No. of letters of appreciation and external
              commendations per 100 police officers.

23   HMIC   Percentage of police officer strength which is female.

24   HMIC   No. of ethnic minority police officers per 1000 ethnic
              minority population.

25(a) A.C.   The number of complaint cases recorded by the
              police force.

25(b) A.C.   The number of complaints recorded from or on behalf of members of the public.

25(c) A.C.   The number of such complaints substantiated.

25(d) A.C.   The number of such complaints resolved informally.

26   ACPO   Percentage of members of Section 106 committees who express satisfaction with police service delivery standards in the aforementioned areas.

27   ACPO   Percentage of Neighbourhood Watch co-ordinators who express satisfaction with support received from the police service.

Resources/Costs

28(a) HMIC   No. of working days lost through sickness per police officer.

28(b) HMIC   Number of working days lost through sickness per civilian employee.

29   A.C.   The number of police officers available for ordinary duty per 1000 population.

30   A.C.   The net expenditure on police per head of population, itemised as follows:-

a) Pay and allowances of constables.
b) Pay and allowances of ranks above constable.
c) Pay of civilian staff.
d) Police pensions and superannuation contributions.
e) Other costs.
f) Less government grant.
g) Net cost to the authority.

Notes

1. The Operational Policing Review (a wide-ranging research
   programme commissioned jointly by the Police Federation,
   Superintendents' Association and Association of Chief Police
   Officers) estimated that by 1989 40 of the 43 police forces in
   England and Wales had implemented some form of management
   by objectives (Joint Consultative Committee 1990).

2. Reports go to Home Office officials, middle-ranking and senior
   officers in the force concerned and to police authority members.
   Outside of these and other police-related categories, circulation
   runs to barely double figures.

3. It states 'The topics deal with areas of obvious potential
   sensitivity involving professional judgement by chief officers in
   implementing the recommendations. The key decisions should be
   made by the force. Chief officer commitment is essential for
   effective implementation. The key phrase is that phase 3 should
   be an audit of *processes*, not *outcomes*. This means, for example,
   that the auditor is not expected to criticise a force for having an
   apparently poor crime clear up rate, but should comment on the
   indicators used by the force to monitor its performance on crime
   detection. In a similar vein, the auditor should not criticise the
   adoption of an objective to reduce domestic burglaries, but
   should instead review the procedures used to set objectives.'

4. As we shall see, monitoring of local opinion more often falls to
   the police than to police authorities. Like the AMA, the
   Commission is aware that the enhanced role it wants for police
   authorities will require more and better officer support and better
   training for members. (See also *We can't go on meeting like this:
   The changing role of local authority members*, Management
   Paper No.8, Audit Commission, 1990).

5. Letter dated 14 August 1991 from the sub-committee's chairman
   to all chief constables.

6. Local authorities are obliged to publish locally the performance information that the Commission specifies: how police authorities choose to present and comment upon the information will clearly be important. The Commission may publish national summaries of this information to facilitate comparisons. It has also undertaken to publish explanatory notes to aid the interpretation of the information.

ACPO has said that it will publish aggregate, national data on public satisfaction but that it will 'not necessarily' publish comparative data (Quality of Service Sub-Committee 1992). It is not clear whether chief constables or police authorities will be free to publish the information for their force. There is, at the time of writing, no indication from the Inspectorate of how its performance indicators are to be published.

7. This list, with some modification, is to be issued as a Home Office circular.

Bibliography

Association of Chief Police Officers (1990) *Strategic policy document. Setting the standards for policing: meeting community expectations.*

Association of Metropolitan Authorities (1991) *The police authority role: Strategic issues.* London.

Audit Commission (Undated) *Audit Guide Phase I Special Study.*

Audit Commission (Undated) *Audit Guide Phase II A & II B Special Study.*

Audit Commission (Undated) *Police Management systems audit guide. Police Audit Phase 3.*

Audit Commission (Undated) *The Citizen's Charter indicators. Charting a course.* London, HMSO.

Audit Commission (1988a) *Administrative support for operational police officers* Police Paper 1, London, HMSO.

Audit Commission (1988b) *Improving the performance of the fingerprint service* Police Paper 2, London, HMSO.

Audit Commission (1988c) *The competitive council* Management Paper 1, London, HMSO.

Audit Commission (1989) *Improving vehicle management in the police service* Police Paper 3, London, HMSO.

Audit Commission (1990a) *Effective policing: performance review in police forces* Police Paper 8, London, HMSO.

Audit Commission (1990b) *Footing the bill: financing provincial police forces* Police Paper 6, London, HMSO.

Audit Commission (1991a) *How effective is the Audit Commission?* London, HMSO.

Audit Commission (1991b) *Reviewing the organisation of provincial police forces* Police Paper 9, London, HMSO.

Audit Commission (1991c) *Pounds and coppers: financial delegation in police forces* Police paper 10, London, HMSO.

Audit Commission (1992) *Citizen's charter performance indicators*, London.

Flannery K (1992) Presentation to AMA Conference 'Minding the quality: police authorities and police performance', November 1992.

HMSO (1982) *Efficiency and effectiveness in the civil service* HC 236, Cmnd 8616, London.

Home Office (1983) Circular 114/1983 *Manpower, efficiency and effectiveness in the police service.*

Home Office (1988) Circular 106/1988 *Applications for increases in police force establishments.*

Inspectorate of Constabulary (1991) *Quality of service: a framework of performance indicators*, mimeo, London.

Joint Consultative Committee (1990) *Operational Policing Review*, Surbiton.

Morgan R (1989) 'Policing by consent': legitimating the doctrine, in Morgan R and Smith D J (eds) *Coming to terms with policing.* London, Routledge.

Peters T J and Waterman R H (1982) *In search of excellence: lessons from America's best-run companies.* New York, Harper and Row.

Pfeffer N and Coote A (1991) *Is quality good for you? A critical review of quality assurance in welfare services.* Social Policy Paper 5. London, IPPR.

Pollitt C (1988) 'Bringing consumers into performance measurement: concepts, consequences and constraints' *Policy and Politics*, 16, 2, 77-87.

Quality of Service Sub-Committee (1991) *Meeting community expectation: 'Making it work', Key Operational Service Areas Performance Indicators*, ACPO.

Quality of Service Sub-Committee (1992) *Performance indicators*, ACPO.

Skogan W G (1990) *The police and public in England and Wales: A British Crime Survey Report* Home Office Research Study 117, London , HMSO.

Walsh K (1991) 'Citizens and consumers: marketing and public sector management'. *Public Money and Management*, 11, 2, 9-16.

Winkler F (1987) 'Consumerism in health care: beyond the supermarket model'. *Policy and Politics*, 15, 1, 1-8.

3. THE LOCAL ACCOUNTABILITY OF POLICE IN ENGLAND AND WALES: FUTURE PROSPECTS
Barry Loveday

In March 1993 the then Home Secretary informed Parliament of the significant changes which the Government proposes to make to the 'management' of the police, changes which are calculated to enhance local autonomy with one hand while strengthening overall central control with the other. Thus, central government control over the allocation of force expenditure is to be devolved to chief constables and their police authorities and a local police authority is for the first time to be established for the Metropolitan Police. The Home Secretary, however, will appoint some of the members of each authority, reducing the proportion of elected councillors to one half, and will have the power to call police authorities to account for the way in which their forces meet nationally set objectives and performance targets.

Police authorities will become free-standing precepting bodies, ending residual local authority control over police expenditure and their ability to balance spending on policing with that on other local services. Police authorities will be expected to set local objectives and performance targets but will apparently have no additional powers to ensure that chief constables attain these targets (other than any indirect control exercised through performance related pay). Devolution of responsibility within forces to local command units is expected to reduce the role of force headquarters to the provision of support services and performance measurement. To avoid the 'unnecessary duplication' of these functions, forces will be amalgamated 'when the time is right'[1].

The Home Secretary acknowledged that the final shape of the new arrangements could not be forseen until the outcome of the current review of local government structure is known. Indeed, the decision by the Government to initiate a major review of the structure of local government was always likely to impinge on the structure of police forces outside the Metropolitan areas. This is now certain to

be the case as the government has indicated a predisposition towards
the elimination of the present two-tier arrangements by which
services are either held or shared between district and county
councils. While the Department of the Environment (DoE) guidance
to the Local Government Commission for England has indicated that
it may wish to retain the existing two-tier system in some areas, the
expectation is that, in most cases, unitary authorities will be
recommended. The DoE bases its argument in favour of unitary
structures on the belief that these will be best able to reflect
community interests and will offer 'the benefit of clarifying
accountability and responsibility' for those services for which local
authorities remain responsible.

Local Government Reorganisation

There is, in fact, much to suggest that the identification of
communities and the creation of single authorities made responsible
for their local services is likely to achieve a high level of public
accountability. Directly elected representatives who are ultimately
responsible for service levels and quality will not be able to use as
a shield the confused lines of accountability which have traditionally
characterised arrangements where services are shared. For these
reasons, amongst others, the commitment to the recreation of unitary
structures is likely to establish a degree of accountability not
experienced since the abolition of the county boroughs by the Local
Government Act of 1972.

It is within the context of the new emphasis placed on local
accountability of services as a policy aim that the specific
recommendations made by the DoE on law and order services must
be viewed. While the Local Government Commission has been
asked to consider arrangements for law and order the DoE guidance
states that:

> 'It is recognised that these services are different in terms of
> funding and accountability and that the prescription should be
> that arrangements should be made, if necessary, for local
> government areas to be combined (as they are in many parts of

the country at present) in order to preserve as far as possible the existing structures for law and order services'[2].

It would appear, therefore, that on the basis of a questionable assumption that the police service is different in terms of accountability, the Commission may propose structures which are distanced from other local services.

In addition to the DoE recommendation, it is the professional view of Her Majesty's Inspectorate of Constabulary (HMIC) that police forces would not be viable for areas smaller than their present boundaries[3]. Although this conclusion can be challenged, the DoE guidance specifies that, where there is a recommendation for an existing county to be replaced by smaller unitary authorities, the Commission:

'will need to consider whether policing needs will best be met by reconstituting the authority as a joint police authority or by amalgamating all or part of it with an adjoining police authority.'[4]

This particular recommendation for police forces appears to contradict the government's professed aim of emphasising local accountability of services. Thus the DoE makes it clear in its guidance to the Commission that:

'statutory joint authorities detract from accountability and the government intend them to be very much the exception.'

As has been argued elsewhere, the difficulties surrounding joint arrangements for services, particularly those for the police, have been amply demonstrated by the Joint Board structures which were created in 1985 by the Local Government Act of that year[5]. There is plentiful evidence to suggest that the government is entirely right in identifying the limitations of such arrangements.

At this time it is unclear how significant the recommendations made by the Local Government Commission will be. Its immediate concern is likely to be those areas with a history of dissatisfaction created by local government reform in 1974, including the restructuring of the counties of Humberside, Cleveland and Avon. Elsewhere, substantial reorganisation becomes more problematic as the unit of local government, particularly for strategic services, would appear to approximate current county boundaries rather than those of districts. If, as is claimed by the DoE, the aim of the Commission is to avoid joint arrangements for services, then this is likely to preclude further decentralisation to district level.

One likely outcome could therefore be the resurrection in the larger conurbations of the all-purpose county borough structures which disappeared in 1974 and, along with this, joint arrangements for strategic services with the hinterlands which surround them. This appears to be the case in relation to the Local Government Commissions' proposals for Derbyshire[6]. If this more limited approach to the reorganisation of local government were to be adopted, then policing arrangements might return to those established after the amalgamations of 1966 and 1968. Following the decision of the then Home Secretary, Roy Jenkins, to combine a large number of small police forces, arrangements were subsequently made to establish joint authorities in those force areas which were considered too small to be viable or effective. Thus for the purposes of the police service, ten county councils have, since 1974, provided joint authorities (as opposed to joint boards) for police forces. West Mercia, Thames Valley, Avon and Somerset and Devon and Cornwall constitute the joint authorities for policing the shire counties. If, as a consequence of future reorganisation, police boundaries no longer coincide with those of the local authority, then arrangements similar to those created in the 1970s could be made to cater for this.

Much depends on how extensive the Commission's recommendations prove to be. If there is a prescription in favour of districts as future unitary authorities, then local government reorganisation can be expected to be more fundamental than anything experienced since 1888. This is, however, unlikely to be the case as the Government has made clear that, while it believes unitary authorities could be the most beneficial structure, there is no recommended standardised unit of local government (in terms of population size or service responsibility) which should be identified by the Commission. The primary purpose would appear to be that the Commission should have regard to the need to establish authority areas such that:

'authorities can carry out their functions effectively and do so in ways which reflect community interests.'[7]

The Association of County Councils argues that the most effective strategic units of authority should continue to be the county with heavily devolved administration of services to a district level. While the Association supports the flexible outcomes in terms of area encouraged by the DoE guidance, it remains strongly committed to a structure of local government which removes the need for joint arrangements because, in its experience, Joint Boards:

'do not measure up to the requirements of accountable local government.'[8]

Experience suggests that, in terms of demonstrating local accountability, joint authorities have nowhere proved to be particularly successful. Removed from the direct influence of individual local authorities, joint authorities have been made responsible for large amorphous boundaries to which there is little local affinity. If, therefore, the objective of local government reorganisation is to enhance local accountability, joint authorities are precisely the opposite of what will bring that about.

National Police Responsibilities

The apparent contradictions which characterise the Government's assessment of structures for local accountability of the police may be explained by a continued ambivalence as to whether the police service constitutes a local service at all. There are, for example, national arrangements for police forces which increasingly impinge on police operations. These include the police national computer organisation, the National Identification Bureau and, most recently, the National Criminal Intelligence Service. Interwoven with a growing national dimension of policing are regional arrangements which extend from regional crime squads to training centres.

In some of the metropolitan areas it would in fact be realistic to describe policing as a regional phenomenon. West Midlands, Greater Manchester and West Yorkshire provide good examples of regional forces which cross numerous district boundaries. West Midlands, crosses seven district council boundaries and Greater Manchester Police crosses ten. There is, additionally, a view within the police service, expressed most recently by the Metropolitan Commissioner[9], that a national police system would be preferable to existing local arrangements as national co-ordination of policing is increasingly necessary. It is perhaps for this reason that assumptions concerning the police held within the DoE appear to preclude this service from serious consideration by the Commission. Yet, as has been consistently argued by successive Home Secretaries, there is no intention or expectation of establishing a national police service; particularly when, in terms of total numbers, that service would now outnumber the British Army[10].

The rejection of a national police system was made explicitly in 1991 by the then Home Secretary, Kenneth Baker, while the importance of local policing was stressed by Kenneth Clarke in his address to the Police Federation Conference in 1992. While their commitment, with hindsight, may have referred more to local *management* (that is, to a local command unit structure), than to local *accountability*, a senior Home Office official stressed publicly in 1992 that, under the tripartite system established by the Police Act 1964, each element of the system had 'a unique contribution to make to policing'[11].

Local Relationships

It was the view of this official that the involvement of the local community through its police authority remained a crucial ingredient in the way the police service was administered. In assessing the composition of the tripartite arrangement consisting of chief constable, Home Office and police authorities, he stated that:

'without the collaborative relationship policing either becomes isolated from the interests of the public or from the views of central or local government or, at the other extreme, it becomes a mere tool of government.'

Although he expressed concern over the limited understanding of the role of the police authority held by the public it was, in his view, important to stress that under the tripartite system, police authorities were not ciphers but existed for a purpose. He concluded that, if counter-action was not taken - and taken by police authorities themselves, there was a danger that they would cease to wield the influence that they should.

Home Secretary's Agenda

Speaking in September 1992 to the Superintendents' Association Conference, however, Kenneth Clarke indicated that he was: 'seriously examining the possibility of major changes in police funding and force boundaries' and that:

'Although he was committed to local involvement in policing, he was not convinced that the current system of police authorities was entirely the best method.'[12]

In making this observation the Home Secretary reiterated views expressed in July 1992 when he indicated that he hoped to bring to the police the same principles of reform which he had adopted for health and education when Secretary of State for those Departments. Commenting on his belief that the way to make a big organisation work effectively was by delegation of responsibility to those 'in charge of doing the job', he went on to add:

'This is not the time to try to explain why I thought doctors and nurses in hospitals should be given more management responsibility, free of day-to-day health authority direction.'[13]

Nor to:

> 'divert to the advantages of giving head teachers and governors complete control of their own affairs, free of local authority control.'

Nevertheless, the overall conclusion was that giving management control to those in charge of operations in a local area remained the primary objective, reflecting a view that similar models for reform could be applied to health, education and the police service. As successively Secretary of State for Health and Education, the Home Secretary had found what he had claimed was an administered system not a managed one[14]. He subsequently initiated a fundamental review of the structure of the police service.[15].

Local Command Units

Home Office proposals for police reorganisation are based upon the introduction of a local command unit (LCU) identified by HMIC and the Audit Commission as the most efficient unit of police organisation. The LCU is now seen as the basic building block of the future police organisation and is planned to replace the two-tier structure of division and sub-division which has characterised most police forces until recently. Introducing the LCU reduces the need for police hierarchies by flattening police management structures. Smaller police units will maximise service delivery and, by cutting overheads, offer a more cost effective service. LCUs may also release resources from within a traditionally centralised service and are expected, if properly resourced and made coherent in terms of service responsibility, to form the basis of a regionalised system of policing. This would offer the opportunity of reducing the overhead costs of numerous headquarters, staffs and bureaucracies. With devolved budgetting and performance measurement, a reduced number of smaller police headquarters could be made responsible for general policing policy and inspection supporting a large number of LCUs. The future structure is one to which HMIC certainly subscribes. It also presents the curious paradox of both simultaneously delegating and further centralising a service. The

LCUs will assume the every day responsibility for policing an area while regional headquarters will determine general policing policy.

One Chief Constable has identified constabulary units of around three to four thousand uniformed personnel as the ideal future size for police forces[16]. It is suggested that the economies of scale, the reduction in the number of forces and greater standardisation of force establishments would allow for a better comparison of performance and assessment of support service requirements. If these proposals were implemented then at least twenty-three local police forces would disappear through amalgamation, the procedure for which will be simplified in the proposed legislative changes[17]. Doubts would arise as to the continued viability of a further seven police forces. This is because at the present time just over sixty percent of police forces in England and Wales have establishments of under two thousand officers.

The decision to move towards implementation of a locally devolved structure of LCUs coincides with the ascendancy within the police service of those who question the value of local government involvement in policing. While there has been, for example, an ongoing debate within local government associations as to the advantages or disadvantages of joint boards, the issue of concern for a minority of senior officers has been the possible elimination of the elected element at local level. Some chief officers have long held the view that local political control represented a threat to police autonomy and operational independence[18]. They have argued for the introduction of police authorities in which members are nominated by the Secretary of State, identifying the Northern Ireland Police Authority as a model for the future on the mainland. The need for elected representatives is considered to become less significant as the primary source of accountability becomes the service delivered by the local command unit with the introduction of national performance measures to which police forces will be obliged to conform.

Some chief officers have argued moreover that the local command unit has 'a natural link to its community based on the Police and

Criminal Evidence Act consultative committees', suggesting the substitution of 'community' interests for those currently represented by locally elected authorities[19]. In May 1991 the then Home Secretary, in addressing the Police Federation, made an interesting substitution in his description of the constituent elements of the tripartite structure. Usually construed as consisting of Home Secretary, police chiefs and police authorities, it was noticeable that in his speech the 'community' replaced the 'police authority' as the third element of the tripartite structure. One conclusion of this recent interest in the community would appear to be that, when the local command units are fully established, the element of local accountability could be considered to be provided by consultative committees on which individuals are of course nominated rather than elected.

At a level above that of the LCU, some chief officers advocated the introduction of police boards on the lines endorsed by the Home Secretary's proposals. These police boards, comprising central and local appointees with a fixed tenure of office would, along with the chief officer, determine policing priorities, standards of service and local performance indicators ' to meet local needs'. In line with the current Home Secretary's view on such appointees, the then Chief Constable of Leicestershire suggested that 'being appointed a member of a board could be seen as a reflection of status and integrity in the community similar to that which is attached to the appointment of Justices of the Peace'[20].

It would appear that for some chief officers, the primary benefit of the police board concept would be the removal of elected members. For these officers, nomination in place of elections would enable the police service to 'shake off local political control' while retaining the best of the tripartite system through police boards and PACE consultative liaison committees. Together these would allow central government to monitor efficiency and effectiveness with predetermined performance indicators and in so doing encourage the movement away from administration to the management of police forces. This would appear to be the model for the Home Secretary's plans. His reformed police authorities will be 'free-standing' with only a loose commitment to local authorities. They would, therefore, closely resemble the Trusts and Boards of Governors which already characterise many public services.

Conflicting Opinions

Although these views may reflect the thinking of the Home Secretary, they are by no means shared by all chief officers and do not appear to represent the views of ACPO. ACPO has challenged some of the underlying assumptions of those who favour further amalgamation and the curtailment of elected authorities[21]. As one Chief Constable has argued recently, most of the present indicators of performance appear to confirm that smaller police forces produce a quality of service which is as good as, if not better, than larger forces[22]. It is the view of many chief officers that the size of a police force needs to be related to the geography and characteristics of the area, its policing problems and 'relationships with other services'. Nor would the creation of ever larger police forces offer solutions to current problems facing the police. In the opinion of one chief officer:

'It would be a disaster to delude ourselves, or the politicians, that a round of further amalgamations will solve our difficulties.'

There was, it was argued, no evidence to suggest that the public wished to be policed by larger, more anonymous police forces or that police officers wanted to be led by remote figures at the head of large constabularies. Nor should the proposal to establish nominated police boards be made without a more detailed evaluation of the consequences of doing so:

'An appointed police board is very attractive from a police management perspective, but would mean that for the first time there was no local police democratic accountability.'

Nor could local police liaison committees be seen as an effective substitute for elected authorities. While liaison committees provide a valuable part of the consultative process, it was his experience that these groups, being non-elected, could often be influenced by small self-interested groups which did not represent the interests of the community. It was his belief that:

> 'No-one can really pretend that the consultative groups provide a mechanism for democratic accountability.'[23]

This Chief Constable's experience only appeared to sustain recent research on the role of local consultative liaison panels. These committees are usually officer-led and do not begin to provide the degree of representation of local interests which has been claimed for them. They might, indeed, be better viewed as a diversion from, rather than a substitute for, local accountability of police. Furthermore, many chief officers conclude that, without the full support of the police, the PACE liaison committees would collapse as a consequence of growing public apathy. These rather weak arrangements would hardly appear to be the structures upon which to place the burden of local police accountability. Additionally, the wider use of nominated members of police boards, may only serve to centralise the police service as a smaller number of chief officers prove ultimately unable to protect the service from growing central direction and departmental interference.

Nominated members of police boards or other authorities are unlikely to enjoy either the authority or legitimacy to enable them to challenge central directives or informal pressures. In this kind of structure any view that the chief officer and his board members could genuinely determine policing priorities must be viewed as unlikely. The over-riding, centrally-determined performance indicators coupled with the veto power held by the central department over member nominations would inevitably mean that local discretion would be limited and subject to government intervention. Voluntarily placing the police service into an effective straight-jacket of central control might be thought a rather curious solution to a perceived problem of local police authority interference. This is particularly the case when it is clear that, at a professional level the police authority role is not viewed as a problem or a threat by many chief officers in the shires or elsewhere. Rather than viewing the police authority negatively, most chief officers recognise the value of an elected authority as one means of identifying and channelling local opinion and matters of local concern. It is for example, the view of one chief constable that:

'From my own experience in provincial forces where there is a direct relationship between a police committee and its parent county body, a common interest can be identified as a true reflection of local opinion.'[24]

Elsewhere, chief officers have supported a continued commitment to the tripartite system which places responsibility for policing at a local rather than a national level. As a result, one conclusion must be that there is no professional consensus concerning a need for radical change of a structure which continues to emphasise the local accountability of the police service. Indeed, as the debate leading up to the Home Secretary's statement to the House of Commons demonstrated, if a consensus exists among chief officers it is one which strongly embraces the local nature of the police service and emphasises policing as a local service made accountable to elected members. This is probably because the police service remains utterly dependent on the support of the local community for its successful operation.

The views expressed by chief officers only strengthen the case for effective local police authorities. If the role of police authorities has diminished over time, this may be explained by their inability to exercise the powers and fulfil the ambiguous responsibilities, given to them by the 1964 Police Act. The operational independence of police, along with a Home Office stance which has traditionally been highly protective of the police, have together frustrated attempts by elected members to act as policy makers rather than ciphers. As will be argued, there are a number of reforms which could radically enhance the police authority role and provide it with an important policy making function.

Home Office Plans

The Government argues that it intends to create 'more powerful and
businesslike police authorities which will give more leadership to
the local police service'. Current Home Office controls on the
allocation of force expenditure will cease, enabling chief constables
'in consultation with their local police authority' to decide on the
right mix of manpower and equipment. The greater autonomy which
police authorities will thus enjoy, including a new police authority
for the Metropolitan Police, will be balanced by giving them
statutory responsibility for the performance of their force, for which
they will be accountable to the Home Secretary. It is not clear how
police authorities are, in turn, expected to hold chief constables to
account for meeting the force objectives and performance targets.

Central control over police authorities will be further enhanced by
the replacement of some elected councillors with members
nominated by the Home Secretary on the basis of the 'skills and
abilities' which are needed to make the authority more
'businesslike'. While those nominated to the boards would be able
to influence the service, it is also clear that the parameters within
which they work would be closely set by the central department.
Financial limits set by the centre, along with funding mechanisms
based on performance-related rewards are themselves quite sufficient
to ensure that the authority would be unlikely to stray too far from
the objectives set by the Home Office and monitored by HMIC. As
the Chairman will also be nominated by the Home Secretary, the
adoption by the police authority of any position contrary to that
identified as appropriate by the Home Office must be unlikely. If
implemented, this would result in a major shift in terms of local
responsibility and influence from elected councillors to government
nominees. Moreover, independence from local government would
mean that the meetings of the authority would not be subject to
local government rules on public access and access to information.

The immediate future for locally elected police authorities and local
responsibility which has traditionally characterised policing in
England and Wales would thus appear to look bleak. This must be

a matter of concern as direct involvement in locally run services encourages responsive management and greater police commitment. If the police in its service role is to be sustained, then local mechanisms of accountability need to be strengthened, rather than weakened; a policy is needed which seeks to complement, rather than replace, accountability through elected representatives with accountability by performance review, customer choice and the Citizens' Charter. The police service will see the erosion of democratic structures which provide some (limited) element of public accountability. Reform will also remove yet another strategic service from local government.

There are a number of options available to those who seek to reverse the trend towards centralisation of the police service and the effective disenfranchisement of the electorate from influence over it. The following proposals are intended to maximise police effectiveness and provide a strong element of public accountability.

Some New Proposals

There is a growing recognition that the concept of 'disaggregation' in public sector management may have some applicability to the management of the police service. Traditionally, the police service has been viewed as a monolithic system within which police officers have the skills, ability and interest to move from a number of tasks to a variety of others at relatively short notice. Yet the classic division of uniform staff from CID, which tends to open up a distinct gulf in what purports to be a unified service, suggests that professional specialisms are sustained over time by those who pursue them. It is sufficient to note that even with 'interchange' and other methods of integration the two distinct functions of criminal investigation and uniformed patrol involve areas of expertise and commitment which are not easily transferable. Although the issue of disaggregation has less applicability at a local level, the breakup of the monolithic police structure may be advantageous in clarifying both professional responsibilities and making lines of accountability for specific functions clearer. In particular, where national co-ordination is necessary, overt national control and accountability

would be preferable to the current arrangements in which national
co-ordination in effect renders local accountability meaningless.

It would be entirely appropriate, for example, to consider the
creation of the National Criminal Information Service (NCIS) in this
light. NCIS, which is expected long-term to take on operational
responsibility for a reduced number of regional crime squads, could
be identified as a National Criminal Investigation Department. As
a national police unit, NCIS could, through its own chief officer, be
made the direct responsibility of the Home Secretary and thus
ultimately accountable to Parliament, its work being scrutinised by
the Home Affairs Committee. Using NCIS as an example, we could
identify other units which have a wider dimension to their function.
This would include Special Branch and the Police National
Computer Organisation, amongst others. The need for clear lines of
accountability suggests that the present confusion as to who is
responsible for these services could best be resolved by the
identification of a single national unit with a line of accountability
to central government.

The explicit recognition of the reality of differing police tasks would
represent a movement towards clearer specificity of function. NCIS
should, for example, be given responsibility for serious crime which
crosses local, or indeed, national boundaries. The advantages of
disaggregation are clear. A National Criminal Investigation arm
would reduce the pressure on smaller police forces to provide
personnel for all contingencies and could also provide the link with
European police systems as European police co-operation develops
in the 1990s. It might begin to develop its status, if that was thought
appropriate, by direct entry on the basis of professional
qualifications and experience; alternatively, an interchange of
personnel with other forces might be more effective in ensuring the
degree of co-operation needed on the ground.

Local Police Forces

The disaggregation of police services would provide the opportunity for locally-based police forces to concentrate on service delivery and the development of inter-agency initiatives which can be expected to play a significant part in future police activity. Local municipal forces could retain the more flexible 'local command unit' and, where possible, have coterminous boundaries with the reformed unitary authorities at local government level.

The location of police forces alongside rather than apart from other local services needs to be emphasised. This is because future policing strategies are likely to encompass much closer collaboration with other services. This will become most explicit in the development of more comprehensive crime prevention programmes. There has been a belated recognition that criminal justice agencies alone are unlikely to make much impact on crime levels necessitating a re-evaluation of the structured collaborative approach to the problem of crime and the development of what is usually described as 'social crime prevention'[25].

There is no evidence to suggest that the police, or any other criminal justice agency, can be expected to make anything but a marginal impact on crime rates. This appears to have been most recently identified in an internal memorandum from the Policy Committee at New Scotland Yard which concludes that rising crime is beyond the control of the police service. The memorandum goes on to argue:

'the truth is that crime trends ... are largely determined by social factors and developments and the propensity of individuals to commit crime depends principally on upbringing, education a host of other social circumstances over which the police have had very little influence in the past and on which we are having a diminishing impact.'[26]

Rather than emphasising crime control, the memorandum supports the view that a more productive approach would be the encouragement of multi-agency collaboration in crime reduction partnerships. This approach could be facilitated by the provision of specific funding for local authorities to develop such partnerships. Local authority initiatives, perhaps co-ordinated by a Community Safety Committee, could also be a useful substitute for the present unrepresentative and largely ineffective consultative arrangements established under PACE 1984. The precise relationship between police forces and their component local command units, on the one hand, and elected police authorities and community safety committees on the other, cannot be specified until the future structure of local government is known. While the elected police authority should ideally be drawn from a local authority whose boundaries are coterminous with that of the police force, the contribution of the Community Safety Committee is needed at the local level, perhaps relating to one single local command unit.

Effective service co-ordination would thus benefit from shared service boundaries established within a local government structure based on unitary authorities. Additionally, the formal links created by inter-agency co-ordination would encourage the reorientation of policing away from 'incident-led' activities towards a 'problem-solving approach' to crime. Problem-solving strategies, as developed within American police forces, require the police to look beyond a particular offence to consider its precipitating causes. This is important because research suggests that few incidents with which the police deal can be construed as isolated events. The incidents to which police respond are usually symptoms of some recurring, underlying problem with which the police are often not concerned. Crime analysis suggests that the problem of crime is usually linked to other (usually) urban problems which will not be solved by police activity based on response to incidents. Given the established links between offences committed and urban problems, the most effective 'police strategy' is likely to be one which works with local services which have the authority to ameliorate specific situations. These services would include environmental health, leisure and amenities, housing and planning departments at a local level.

A problem-solving approach to policing, developed within a wider context of social crime prevention, is likely to prove most fruitful in terms of crime reduction. The problem of reorientating policing in this way should not be underestimated. Recent research in Holloway, London, has for example demonstrated that 'sector policing' can be painful initially for the police organisation to develop[27]. In this context police effectiveness would be judged by the extent to which the service was able to support inter-agency co-operation. This might be encouraged by a statutory requirement placed on local authority services and the police to report to a local Community Safety Committee responsible for crime prevention co-ordination. Given the sometimes conflicting objectives within local services, statutory rather than voluntary arrangements may prove to be more influential and productive.

Constabulary Independence

One consequence of the present government's review of police is likely to be a challenge to the concept of constabulary independence to which the police service has remained wedded since the 1920s. The likely introduction of senior appointments from outside the service, when coupled with fixed contracts of employment and the application of national performance measures, will inevitably undermine the convention. If, as is expected, private sector provision begins to assume a greater significance, then it will be the purchaser of services which will, in future, be making decisions on the provision of services, not the provider of that service. This is significant if only because police forces have traditionally 'managed themselves' by deciding levels of service provided to the public and how those resources are used to achieve those objectives set by them. The logic of managed services encouraged by the present Home Secretary must ultimately present a significant challenge to the professional control over the police service exercised until now by senior police officers.

That said, it is not yet clear whether the Government plans, as in other public services, to complete the purchaser - provider split by giving the police authority control over the way in which the budget is allocated. Rather, the Home Secretary said that 'Chief constables will in future have greater freedom to manage their resources. In consultation with their police authority, they will be able to decide on the right mix of manpower and equipment needed...'[28]. What is clear, however, is that police officers will be required to achieve specified targets set by senior officers, police authorities and the Home Secretary. Moreover, performance-related pay could increasingly erode the wide discretion which senior police officers have traditionally exercised.

Social Markets

The need to extend the division between purchasers and providers of services has been stressed by Howard Davies, the former Director of the Audit Commission, now Director General of the CBI. In an important monograph Davies specifically recommends the introduction of components which together would provide successful social markets for public services. These include, *inter alia*, a rational financial framework, clearly defined outputs and a clear division between the purchaser and provider of services. It is Davies' opinion that the accountability of police and responsibility for service provision are confused by present arrangements (a confusion which, it appears, is perpetuated in the Home Secretary's proposals). It is also his view that the police service is a public service most in need of reform along social market lines.

There are understandable misgivings about a social market approach which so clearly fails to engage those values associated with local democracy. There must also be some doubt about an approach which does not recognise local government as an important forum of community aspirations. Nevertheless, there are features in the social market model identified by Davies which could have a significant application in improving the local accountability of police. It is worth identifying the major components of his model:

1.   A rational financial framework.
2.   Clearly defined outputs.
3.   A purchaser/provider split.

4. Market testing and competing providers.
5. Contracts.
6. Customer choice.
7. A strong and realistic customer voice.
8. Comparative data on performance.
9. A strong lay management.
10. Independent inspection and audit[29].

In a reformed police structure there would, for example, be a good case for clearly identifying the police authority as the purchaser of services. The authority would thus be involved in market testing and assessing the potential service of competing providers where this was considered appropriate. If, as seems likely, police services are put out to tender under Compulsory Competitive Tendering (CCT) or by market testing, then it would be entirely appropriate for the police authority to act as purchaser. The division between purchaser and provider in terms of the police service would almost certainly revitalise the role of the police authority which, as the Home Secretary proposes, would be responsible for monitoring levels of service and developing comparative data on performance. The status of the police authority could be enhanced in a social market setting where a significant emphasis was placed on strong lay management. Lay management might also provide the opportunity for police authorities to begin to fulfil those statutory duties originally placed upon them by the Police Act 1964. This has always been difficult in a service controlled by professional chief officers whose statutory authority gives them responsibility for the 'direction and control' of their force.

Under the Police Act 1964 police authorities are already required by statute to provide an 'adequate and efficient' police force. One consequence of this is that police authorities should easily be able to accommodate those responsibilities which the purchaser of services exercises in a social market setting. Additionally, existing police inspection teams, which now report internally to police forces, might instead be made directly responsible to the police authority as purchaser of police services. Independent inspection at local level could prove to be a useful complement to the national inspectorate role which appears likely to become an increasingly 'civilianised' function.

The financing of police forces will need separate consideration. For a variety of reasons it is important that a strong element of police finance remains local. This would be necessary to emphasise the local nature of policing and also to sustain the independent status of the police authority as a service purchaser. Ideally, one central government department should be made responsible for the bulk of funding while perhaps one third of police spending is generated locally. This division of responsibility would enhance both the authority and legitimacy of the police authority and its elected representatives. It would also overcome the evident problems which have surrounded the joint central responsibility for police finance, shared until now between the Home Office and the Department of the Environment.

Within a liberal democracy, there can be no justification for the former Home Secretary's view that greater financial autonomy can only be delegated to 'local' police authorities which are effectively controlled from the centre by a nomination process. This procedure allows the selection of individuals with views which the Home Secretary, rather than the local electorate, considers acceptable. The relaxation of financial control which is proposed will only be of value if representatives of the community are able to exercise a judgement on spending and on policy which is independent, on occasion, of the Secretary of State. The full ramifications of the proposed national police objectives and performance indicators have yet to be understood. Together they could represent, in the hands of a centralising government, a major threat to the local responsibility for policing and to the ability of a local police authority to exercise an independent judgement.

Conclusion

There are a number of strands identified in this paper which when brought together offer a radical and coherent alternative to the proposals put forward by the present Home Secretary for police forces in England and Wales. These include the disaggregation of the police service and the explicit recognition that specific tasks may be carried out more effectively by the creation of dedicated units; and the creation of a national operational detective arm with responsibility for serious offences which cross regional and national boundaries, relieving existing forces of some of the pressure for further amalgamations. This in turn would emphasise the local policing role, reinforced by the retention of police forces whose boundaries coincide with those of the local authority, and inter-agency Community Safety Committees at local command unit level. Separating units of service by function can enhance the work of each unit and it is of interest here that in Europe the development (particularly in France) of municipal police forces by local authorities has proved to be both workable and successful[30].

Precisely what the police authority does decide should reflect local needs and local priorities, informed by, among other means, their Community Safety Committees and consultative committees. The authority should be a wholly elected body and also a purchaser of services. The social market approach provides a useful mechanism to enable an elected authority to overcome the problems traditionally associated with a service dominated by its chief officers. Clearly, the national performance measures and close oversight which the Home Secretary plans to exercise on the basis of the comparative data provided by police authorities will effectively circumscribe the degree of police independence which chief officers have in the past traditionally exercised. Fixed contracts awarded by police authorities whose chairman is personally appointed by the Home Secretary are also likely to erode the autonomy of chief officers. Additionally, where in future those who are appointed to head police forces are drawn from civilian and private sector backgrounds, the convention of constabulary independence is likely to be further limited.

Some police services are likely to be contracted out. These competing providers are likely to be discovered within the private sector and the involvement most recently of Group 4 security and other private companies in the provision of prison services would appear to be the precursor of a similar development within policing. Nevertheless, it should be for the police authority not the police force to decide whether such contractual arrangements continue or whether the service is provided in-house.

The development of the police authority towards the role of purchaser of services would not therefore represent a further radical departure. It would, however, for the first time emphasise the importance of an agency other than the police deciding service objectives. Within this context, some operational independence will rightly be retained. It would not, for example, be the responsibility of the police authority to dictate to police in detail how the objectives are achieved.

As a purchaser of services the local police authority will need management support services. It will need resources to be able to assess and analyse comparative data on performance and develop effective information systems upon which management decisions can be made. This in effect is what the local police authority should be doing anyway. If the application of independent inspection and audit is applied as recommended by those who propose social markets then they will be in a position to exercise a real judgement as to the overall efficiency and effectiveness of the police service for which they have statutory responsibility.

Notes

1. House of Commons, 23 March 1993.

2. DoE Guidance to the Local Government Commission for England: Draft for Consultation. November, 1991, para. 9.

3. DoE Guidance, para 23.

4. DoE Guidance, para. 23.

5. B Loveday, 'The New Police Authorities' in *Policing and Society*, Vol. 1., 1991.

6. The *Independent*, 16 March 1993: 'Derbyshire split points way for local government'.

7. DoE Guidance, para. 6.

8. Speech by Mr R Wendt to ACPO Conference, 10 June 1992.

9. Sir Peter Imbert, Police Foundation Annual Lecture. Guildhall. 1991.

10. Home Secretary to Police Foundation Annual Lecture, Guildhall, 1991.

11. Mr Ian Burns, Home Office. ACPO Conference, June 1992.

12. The *Independent*, 21 September 1992.

13. The *Guardian*, 2 July 1992.

14. *Ibid*.

15. The *Guardian*, 2 July 1992.

16. Michael Hirst, then Chief Constable of Leicestershire Constabulary. *Police*, August 1992.

17. House of Commons Debates, 23 March 1993.

18. eg. see Ian Oliver, (1987) *Police, Government and Accountability.* Macmillan (Ch.17).

19. Again see Ian Oliver, *ibid.*

20. Michael Hirst, *Police*, August 1992.

21. eg. as argued by Tony Coe at the ACPO Summer Conference, Eastbourne, 1992.

22. Raymond White, *Police*, September, 1992.

23. *ibid.*

24. Mr A T Coe, Suffolk Constabulary. Speech to ACPO Conference, 10 June 1992.

25. J Bright and N Whiskin, *Police*, October 1992.

26. *The Observer*, 4 April 1993.

27. See 'Serving the People. Sector policing and public accountability', Dixon and Stanko, Brunel University, 22 April 1993.

28. Commons Debate, 23 March 1993, col.766.

29. Howard Davies, *Fighting Leviathan: building social markets that work*, Social Market Foundation, London 1992.

30. Gleizal J, Gatti-Domenach J and Journes C. (1993) *La Police, La cas des democracie occidental.* Press Université de France.

4. CONTROLLING THE DISCRETION OF THE INDIVIDUAL OFFICER
Andrew Sanders

Robert Reiner showed in his chapter that the purpose of accountability is to control policing policy and, by requiring the police to account for their actions, to control policing more effectively in the future. This is as applicable in relation to the types of police decision discussed in this chapter (categorised by Reiner as the 'use of legal powers') as any other. However, accountability in both senses is more limited in effectiveness here than in such matters as policing style or personnel management. This is because, first, the particular personnel policy which is adopted, for instance, is presumably desired by the police organisation (even if not by individual officers). Hence police management has an interest in control and review which it may not have in relation to externally imposed controls on the exercise of legal powers. Second, as Reiner points out, the doctrine of constabulary independence impinges on the use of legal powers. Third (again highlighted by Reiner) the use of these powers are low visibility decisions.

A realistic policy of, and structure for, accountability for individual decisions has therefore to acknowledge the fact of operational discretion. To the extent that discretion has to remain, our attention should focus not only on ways to control it but also on what areas of discretion are feasible to control. The following discussion focuses on selected areas of individual discretion. Many issues not discussed - eg. identification parades, entry search and seizure, surveillance, intimate searches and the taking of intimate samples - raise identical issues and the analysis should apply to all discretionary powers.

Street Policing

We are concerned here with policing which leads to the apprehension of suspects. Apprehended suspects are usually arrested and taken to the police station. They may, however, 'volunteer' to attend the police station without arrest, or may talk 'voluntarily' with the officer. Apprehension may be preceded by surveillance and may have been by way of stop and search, but neither is necessary. Prosecution, when it occurs, is nearly always preceded by arrest, even of those who initially 'volunteered' to attend the station.

Academic research shows·that most police arrests do not derive from proactive policing. They are citizen initiated, in the sense that most crimes are reported by victims to the police (and so are not discovered by police efforts, alone) and many arrestees are 'fingered' by victims. This has led some researchers (eg. Steer, 1980) to suggest that the role of police discretion in arrest decisions is minimal, but this misreads the situation for information from citizens has to be sifted, evaluated and acted upon by the police. In one study (Black, 1970) only two thirds of citizen complaints were taken seriously by the police. Even if complaints are acted on and suspects identified, arrest is not automatic. Indeed, for many offences (eg. minor public order offences and domestic violence) arrest is less than usual. Hence the factors governing police discretion in their proactive mode also structure the actions òf the police when acting on information from citizens (McConville *et al* 1991, ch.2).

Police street work is inquisitorial, ie. fact-finding. Many arrests arise purely by chance or from the police seeking viable suspects for a particular offence rather from an initial construction of a case against a particular individual. Rarely are arrests ordered, or supervised, by senior officers (Maguire and Norris, 1992). Stops and arrests (and the evidence on which they are based) are thus of 'low visibility'.

Stops and arrests should be based on 'reasonable suspicion'[1] which need not satisfy the evidential standards of a court. Many legitimate stops and arrests, then, will be based on evidence in need of supplementation (eg. through police station interrogation, identification by witnesses, fingerprint evidence etc) before a prosecution can be initiated. Hence such evidence can legitimately be 'thin'.

Clearly the police currently have enormous discretion in street policing. But street policing is not arbitrary. It is structured - in the absence of either complete legal rules, or precise and workable legal rules - by the police's own informal working rules ('informal norms'). The three most important are the previous convictions of suspects known to local officers (Smith and Gray 1983; McConville *et al* 1991, Ch.2); the maintenance of order and police authority (Sanders 1988a; McConville *et al* 1991, Ch.2); and general 'suspiciousness', such as being in 'the wrong place at the wrong time', the way the suspect was moving or loitering, and so forth (Matza, 1969; Willis, 1983; Dixon *et al*, 1989).

Police officers were often unable to specify, when interviewed by researchers (such as Willis and McConville *et al*), why they stopped and searched large proportions of their suspects, both in cases where evidence leading to arrest and charge was discovered and where it was not. Officers would talk about 'instinct' or 'something undefinable'. Insofar as policing is a craft rather than a rule-bound mechanical job this is not surprising, for the essence of artistry and craft is the use of imagination and the creative application of rules and experience.

Patterns of class and race bias are one result of the weak constraint of legal rules (Smith and Gray 1983). Disproportionate numbers of black people, for instance, are stopped, searched, and arrested (Willis, 1983; Jefferson and Walker, 1992). These British findings are consistent with those of American research where legal rules and criminal justice processes are similar. When black or, to a lesser extent, working class people are not in their own areas the police notice this. Disproportionate numbers of these groups have criminal records, create disorder, and challenge the police (or are so perceived by the police). Insofar as they perceive themselves to be unfairly harassed by the police, as Lord Scarman (1981) acknowledged, this would not be surprising.

Existing controls

1. *Offence definition*:

Arrest can be only for suspicion of a specific offence, but many offence definitions are too vague for this to be an adequate control (eg. offensive weapon, drunk and disorderly, breach of the peace, disorderly conduct, going equipped for theft, and even burglary). Thus the police may arrest someone carrying their work tools where they may have legitimate reasons for carrying them or where they may indeed be guilty of two of the above offences. Conclusive evidence will often be obtainable only through confession since guilt or innocence turns on the intent of the suspect which can often be ascertained in no other way. Pinning down what made an officer sufficiently suspicious to stop and then arrest a suspect in such circumstances is inevitably difficult.

2. *Police powers of stop and arrest*:

As stated earlier, 'reasonable suspicion' is ill-defined. Neither judges in Appeal cases nor the legislature have sought to define it at all. Thus arrest can be based upon undefined suspicion about an object whose purpose is ambiguous!

3. *Home Office Guidance*:

Codes of Practice made under PACE attempt to restrict discretion in key areas, namely stop and search (and, by implication, arrest) and entry search and seizure (where similar problems of 'reasonable suspicion' arise). The guidance here is primarily negative though, stating what does not amount to 'reasonable suspicion' (hair style, ethnic group, and so forth). This reflects the impossibility of positively defining the concept. The Code insists that the factors exciting suspicion must be objective - ie. something of which a reasonable third party could take cognisance.

4. *Written records*:

One of PACE's main innovations, which formed the centre-piece of the Royal Commission on Criminal Procedure's schema, is reliance on written records of police handling of suspects. Thus records must be made of stop and search made under S.1 PACE, and must be made available to the suspect on request. However, since the record is made by the officer concerned there is no guarantee that the encounter will be recorded faithfully. Further, 'consensual' searches are not made under S.1 PACE and therefore do not require records to be made. Dixon *et al* (1990b) found that the police generally prefer to regard stops (and search of premises) as consensual largely for this reason. Whether the subjects of such stops and searches generally see them in this way is doubtful, for 'consent' in conditions of coercion and power is largely illusory.

5. *Supervision*:

As stated earlier, direct supervision is very rare. Most supervision consists of checking paperwork - ie. the records made by the officers being supervised.

The Scope for Control

What is striking about the research findings on which this discussion has been based is that the research done after the introduction of PACE (Eg. Dixon *et al*, 1989, 1990b; McConville *et al*, 1991) has produced very similar results to that conducted prior to PACE (Eg Smith and Gray, 1983; Willis, 1983). Policing practice appears to be little changed. As one officer told McConville *et al*, he would still stop a suspect 'instinctively and then think about how he would satisfy a third party'. This suggests that the Codes and requirements of written records have done far more to change the way officers *account* for their exercise of discretion than to the way they *actually* exercise it. In other words, police working rules (and therefore the practices that flow from them) remain substantially unaltered. This is hardly surprising, given that controls 1 and 2 (above) and the inquisitorial role of the police at this stage are unaltered.

How the police exercise discretion, and whom they exercise it upon, is thus poorly uncontrolled. Some groups are disproportionately subjected to stop and arrest powers. This is partly because of vague laws. But it is also because the actual evidence on which decisions are made, and the exercise of them, are of extremely low visibility. Further, constabulary independence would limit the extent to which supervision could be effective even were other conditions different.

To exercise more control, little can be done to make controls 3, 4 and 5 more effective; it is difficult to think of any effective new controls, and the inquisitorial role of the police cannot be altered. We are left with controls 1 and 2. As to the first, vague offences should certainly be abolished (many would not survive the US Supreme Court's constitutional rules, for instance, as Lustgarten, 1987 points out). As to the second, to require more evidence prior to arrest could have two undesirable effects.

First, it would bring forward to this stage the adversarial role occupied by the police at later stages because the police would have to identify prosecutable suspects prior to arrest. In a fight, for instance, the police might currently arrest all the protagonists in order to discover who was responsible. It would be undesirable to alter arrest requirements which would have the effect of requiring them to decide on the street, on the basis of inadequate information in the heat of the moment, who was to blame. The police mind should be encouraged to be as open as possible for as long as possible. Since excessive adversarialism is often seen as a major cause of miscarriages of justice one might want to make the police less (rather than more) adversarial, at this stage at any rate.

Second, putting pressure on the police to secure more evidence prior to arrest would entail them collecting yet more evidence in conditions of low visibility. Interrogation prior to the formal interrogation would become more common. If one wishes the extraction of information from suspects to be more, rather than less, visible one might want to require the police to secure *less* - rather than more - evidence than now in order to arrest (and then to compensate for this one might want to require more evidence than now to hold suspects in detention for more than, say, four hours).

One is left with the conclusion that street policing is of such low visibility that attempts to control it substantially beyond that which come naturally to the police would be both undesirable and impractical. It might be better to attempt to control it only minimally, because it could have the unintended negative effects discussed above. To control this less, ie. to concede more powers to the police, might then make it easier for the police to accept more controls in areas where they would be more meaningful.

The Suspect in the Police Station

Once an arrest has been made and a suspect brought to the police station, the police are in adversarial (as distinct from inquisitorial) mode. Their task is to secure evidence against suspects, rather than dispassionately to seek 'the facts' about an incident. Most suspects are interviewed (interrogated), which often produces statements which the police may then check (eg. alibi evidence) or seek to discredit (eg. by scientific evidence). Most important, the police seek confession evidence from interrogation, which in fact forms the basis of most prosecuted cases (McConville and Baldwin, 1981).

The police continue to operate their working rules. To the extent that 'suspicious' people or those who are disorderly or 'known' to the police are arrested without reasonable suspicion, the police seek to find evidence to fit a charge. Charges are therefore sometimes a resource for the police to justify arrest and further detention (Sanders 1985). Because of the way the police 'construct' interrogations and evidence in general, and their overwhelming adversarial rather than truth-seeking stance, evidence is often unreliable (McConville *et al* 1991). Evidence of guilt through interrogation is secured in many ways:

1. The desire of many suspects - perhaps the majority - to confess.

2. Intimidation and 'tactics' (see eg. Irving and Mckenzie 1989; Maguire and Norris, 1992; Evans 1992). Many tactics and forms of implicit intimidation (such as threatening long stays in the cells: Sanders *et al* 1989) are lawful. Extreme tactics are not and thus they have disappeared from formal interrogations. But even lawful tactics are often intimidating to particularly vulnerable people (Gudjonsson and McKeith, 1982), and even 'ordinary' people are vulnerable to tactics producing 'coerced-passive' confessions (McConville *et al*, 1991, Ch.4).

3. Informal interrogation: Interrogations not tape recorded will be recorded manually by an officer (or not) and may therefore include unrecorded unlawful tactics such as threats or inducements. (Sanders and Bridges, 1990; McConville, 1992)

4. 'Gilding the Lily': the falsification of a confession. See Kaye's discussion of the Serious Crime Squad cases (1991) and, more generally, Holdaway (1983).

Existing Controls

The adversarial role of the police at this stage, and the inherent power imbalance between police and suspect when detained, is implicitly recognised by the existence of legislative controls. PACE, in particular, provides various rights for suspects and protection for them against the police (many more than are available to suspects on the street). The assumption behind these controls is *not* that, without them, the police would be literally uncontrolled. It is that on *some* occasions the police need control. There is no reason to doubt that many or most suspects are treated entirely properly by the police. As stated earlier, many suspects confess simply because they wish to. The controls are needed in relation to those - be they many or few - who make damaging statements involuntarily.

Accountability at this stage should seek to ensure that the police behave fairly in three ways:

a. according to absolute notions of fairness;
b. according to the law; and
c. in respect of the equal treatment of different groups of suspects.

The most important controls are:

1. *Detention*:

Initial detention is allowed only when it is considered 'necessary' by the custody officer (PACE S. 37), but in fact it is almost never refused (McKenzie 1990; McConville *et al* 1991, Ch 3). The institution of the custody officer (CO) is itself supposed to be a protection for suspects as the CO is supposedly independent of the police, but research shows COs - not surprisingly - to be torn between their outlook as police officers and their protective role. Thus, although they generally carry out their pure 'welfare' role conscientiously (providing proper meals, rest periods and so forth), this is not true of other aspects of the role (such as periodic reviews of detention) (see eg. Dixon *et al* 1990a).

Of course, it is dangerous to over-generalise. Custody officers vary in their preparedness to apply the Codes of Practice strictly. However, experienced officers get to know which custody officers are 'all PACE, PACE, PACE' and which are not. Thus it has been suggested that they can control when they make an arrest and, often, which stations suspects are brought to, enabling 'awkward' custody officers to be by-passed. As we have seen, none of this is necessary in relation to most suspects. But when it is thought necessary, experienced officers have the means of evading this particular control. After all, if some officers were not thought able and willing to use dubious tactics against some suspects some of the time, the institution of the CO would not have been invented in the first place.

2. *Access*:

Access to solicitors and friends/relatives may be delayed in exceptional circumstances but never refused altogether (PACE S 58). In particular, suspects must be offered free legal advice and their entitlement clearly explained to them. The obligation on the police is greater under the revised Code of Practice (issued in 1991) than hitherto and unpublished figures suggest that, as a result, the numbers securing advice have risen greatly: from less than 10 per cent before PACE to around 20 per cent in 1987-8, and now nearer 30 per cent (Sanders and Bridges, 1992). Nonetheless, Sanders and Bridges showed that:

● the fact that there are far more suspects who refuse advice than who do not means that these protection are far from universal.

● prior to the revised Code the police used many 'ploys' (some illegal, some not) to dissuade suspects from securing advice, and there is no reason to believe that these ploys are not still used. Again, this is not to suggest that the majority of suspects are subjected to such ploys or that they amount to *denial* of access. But, again, attempts to evade controls are most likely to occur in precisely those situations for which the controls were designed.

● interviewing prior to access or between solicitors' visits takes place, thus negating the value of the access. Again, the point here is not that this 'informal' interviewing routinely occurs, but that officers can secure it when they feel they need to do so.

● legal advice does not necessarily protect suspects from police tactics, either because it is provided only over the telephone or because the solicitor is not sufficiently adversarial.

The fact that increasing numbers of suspects secure advice and that increasing numbers of suspects are treated properly by the police (including less recourse to interrogation 'tactics') should not lead us into the 'quantitative fallacy': the point is not how many suspects are manipulated or denied legal protection, but whether the police are able to use the pressures and evasions of the law which they need to use, on the suspects who matter to them, to achieve their purposes. Whilst accountability for police station practices is as rudimentary as it is at present there is no reason to doubt the capacity of some police officers in this respect.

3. *Tape recording of interrogations*:

The purpose of this is to ensure that the interrogation record is accurate and that suspects are not improperly pressured (access to solicitors having, *inter alia*, the same purpose). Informal interrogation, especially prior to police station detention, is not allowed (except in exceptional circumstances) precisely for these reasons. But tape recording is of limited value. Scenic routes, allowing police car interrogations to occur, increase (McConville and Morrell, 1983; Maguire and Norris, 1992); other informal interrogations occur outside the interrogation room or in the cell (Sanders and Bridges, 1990; McConville, 1992); and police summaries of tape recorded interrogations are distorted (Baldwin and Bedward, 1991). Video recording will suffer in the same ways.

The release by the Court of Appeal of the 'Cardiff Three' in 1992 is a case in point. It is true that their release was due to the intimidation and coercion, as revealed by tape recordings, which they suffered when repeatedly interrogated by the police. However, these tapes did not prevent their initial convictions for murder; and presumably neither their defence solicitor (who was present at their interrogations) nor the police considered this coercion to be anything unusual. The defendants and solicitor could have given evidence to the Court of Appeal - or the original trial court - about the interrogations without any tape recordings. The same result would have ensued as long as the police had been honest about the way they carried out the interrogation.

The 'Cardiff Three' case shows that at least some police officers are prepared to behave, in front of tape recorders and defence solicitors, in ways which the Court of Appeal finds unacceptable. The obvious implication is that they are prepared to carry on in such ways through informal interrogations which are not tape recorded and not in the presence of legal advisors.

4. *Custody Record*:

Like records of stop and search, these record what should have happened as much as what did happen. This makes them as much a protection for police officers as a way of making those officers account for their actions. Sanders and Bridges (1990), for instance, found that - in relation to access to legal advice alone - over 10 per cent of custody records were falsely completed. McConville (1992) found not only that a CO allowed a police officer unlawful access to a suspect in his cell to interrogate him informally, but that there was no record of this in the custody record. The value of custody records, as with records of interrogation and information to suspects about their rights, depends in part on the attitude of the custody officer which is not uniform. As stated earlier, however, zealous custody officers can often be by-passed by officers who wish to do so.

5. *Supervision by senior officers*:

Again, most supervision is of the paperwork, such as custody records or interrogation notes/transcripts rather than of actual reception into custody or the conduct of interrogation. Moreover, McConville's (1992) unlawful cell interrogation was actually *by the senior officer*, and Maguire and Norris (1992) acknowledge that, as far as the CID is concerned, officers often learn how to circumvent rules from senior colleagues. Again, in the 'Cardiff Three' case, the senior officer refused to condemn the tactics used by his subordinates.

6. *Right of silence*:

This is rarely exercised, though more when access is secured than not (although demonstrating a causal connection is difficult). Given the failure of the controls detailed above, the failure to exercise silence in most cases is not surprising. Indeed, according to the Code of Practice, the job of the police is to seek answers to questions even if the suspect asserts his intention not to answer. This means the police's job is to put pressure on suspects to change their minds, and in this they are often successful. Most suspects are released after less than eight hours detention. But detention is allowed for 24 hours (extendable in serious cases). This gives a lot of time for re-interviews and the general pressure of involuntary custody to operate, especially as getting out of the cells as quickly as possible is the number one priority for most suspects (Sanders *et al* 1989).

The Scope for Control

Control can only begin to be effective if we observe the logic of a fundamental equation: that if the police are trying to fulfil their legitimate role, inhibiting them from doing it in one forum will encourage them to do it in another. Thus banning threats, 'inducements' and informal 'chats' in 'real' interrogations has pushed these things into informal interrogations, which are less controlled and visible than ever. Similarly, the rules on interrogation effectively require it to occur in a police station, while the rules on detention attempt to reduce police station detention and thus police station interrogation. The result is 'voluntary' attendance in breach of PACE and 'rubber stamping' of the detention rules. For the pressure to secure confessions through interrogation takes priority over the pressure to be law abiding.

Control is therefore possible only in certain limited ways, as follows:

1. By reducing the pressure to detain and to interrogate: this would necessitate changing substantive laws requiring proof of 'intent' or 'recklessness'. This might create more problems than it would solve in extending criminal liability, and it would not remove all pressures to interrogate. It also might be a case of the 'tail wagging the dog', for the advantages of current policy on intent (preventing criminal liability for negligent actions in most non-motoring situations, for instance) might outweigh the unfortunate propensity to interrogate which it creates.

2. By rendering valueless the products of unlawful behaviour (unlawful interrogation, unlawful denial of access to legal advice, unlawful stops and arrests etc) and making all products of 'chats' inadmissible through an exclusionary rule. But many problems will remain (Sanders 1988b), including proving that the unlawful events occurred in the first place.

3. By defence agents or neutral agents policing police stations - eg. permanent duty solicitors or custody clerks, or interrogation by magistrates. The civilianisation of custody officers, which is currently being considered, might be helpful here. However, any person or institution operating this kind of role is in danger of being 'captured' by police ideology.

4. By simply rendering the products of interrogation less important by preventing conviction on confession evidence alone. This would entail introducing a corroboration rule, as in France (Leigh and Zedner, 1992).

Prosecution Decisions

Despite the introduction of the Crown Prosecution Service (CPS) in 1986, the police still decide whether or not to initiate prosecutions in most cases. If they do decide to prosecute, the case is handed over to the CPS which can decide without reference to the police whether to continue and (if they do) whether to stay with the charges chosen by the police. Thus, in any particular case the police may decide to take no further action (NFA) (around 40 per cent of all adult cases), caution (around 10 per cent of all adult cases) or prosecute (most of the rest). The institutional arrangements are somewhat different for juveniles but not significantly so in principle or practice in relation to the ability of the police to control events (Evans and Ferguson, 1991; McConville *et al* 1991, Ch.7)

In this role the police are distinctly adversarial, their role being to make out a case. They would be wrong not to act accordingly, for they are still the prosecutors and, as such, it is their duty to prosecute only in cases which (through their own efforts) are strong.

Current Controls

1. *Decisions not to prosecute*:

The police are accountable, in theory, for their prosecution decisions to the courts and to the CPS. In reality they are of course accountable to neither, for decisions not to prosecute (largely no further action (NFA) caution) end with the police. Like street work, this police work is of very low visibility and 'constabulary independence' allows the accumulation of individual decisions to distort policy. Thus a policy always to prosecute or always to caution/NFA can distort strategic policies about the types of offence to police. For example, patterns of prosecution and caution for drugs possession, vice, and domestic violence go through periodic 'highs' and 'lows'.

Decisions to caution, as distinct from taking no action at all, are not simply 'let offs'. Hence Home Office guidelines set out preconditions for caution aimed at ensuring the guilt of the suspect, but these are often ignored by the police (McConville *et al* Ch 7; Evans 1991). Since cautions may be cited in (juvenile) court and are used to justify future decisions to prosecute (as indeed are NFAs), they are of great importance.

2. *Decision to prosecute*:

The Attorney-General's Guidelines on Prosecution (1983) and the Code for Crown Prosecutors set out evidential and public interest tests which should be satisfied before the police (and CPS) prosecute. The police are accountable to the CPS and the courts for prosecutions which breach these guidelines but court and CPS controls are weak for several reasons:

a.   A failure to perceive breaches of guidelines. The police ability and desire to 'construct' evidence to support arrest, detention and charge is an inevitable product of their control over police-suspect encounters and their adversarial stance. It is, in other words, their job to make their cases as strong as possible, and to ignore, undermine, or discount evidence which would point to acquittal or non-prosecution in the 'public interest'. Thus when the Code is breached the police seek to hide this, often successfully (McConville *et al* 1991, Ch 7, 8).

The CPS does drop evidentially weak cases, and so construction is not always successful. In this sense there is some accountability; but cases are not really dropped because of breaches. They are dropped because they are likely to end in acquittal, which is by no means all evidentially weak cases. The CPS, like the police, seeks to win, which is not the same as doing justice.

Courts, in particular, are usually ill-placed to judge the propriety of most prosecutions since their task is to adjudicate on what is presented to them not to assess whether they should have been presented with less, more, or different evidence. Neither courts nor CPS can judge, on the basis of police evidence alone, whether most cases are in the 'public interest' (Stone, 1989).

b. Unwillingness to communicate displeasure. While there are occasions when courts express displeasure at hopeless cases being brought, the prosecution of cases not in the 'public interest' is rarely, if ever, criticised. Indeed, most courts regard judgement of the public interest as their province and not that of the police. One magistrate - an academic criminologist - told me that although he criticises the police for prosecuting such cases, his colleagues do not. Similarly, the CPS very rarely object to the prosecution of such cases. Why should they in an adversarial system when such cases end in conviction for them?

c. Inability to apply sanctions. Being found in breach of a Code or guideline has no significant consequences for police officers. Even if there is criticism it is very rarely public or comes to the attention of supervising officers.

The Scope for Control

Low visibility, even in prosecuted cases (due to the hidden and subtle processes of case construction) makes control difficult. Explanatory accountability (explaining the reasons after the event) in individual cases would be invidious if it was done in public. In any event, to be meaningful, the explanations would have to be verifiable which would require confidential police files to be opened up to whoever the police were accountable to.

Before deciding the direction of reform, what it is that one wants to control has to be decided: unfettered prosecution, with the attendant costs and strains for defendant and system alike? Or unfettered diversion? Currently, the interests of victims, defendants, the State and the police themselves may all diverge in particular cases. Cautions are supposed to be in the defendant's interest, 'taking into account' that of the victim. Often neither's interest is taken into account. Cautions can be tools for getting informants back onto the street, keeping tabs on suspects, justifying arrest and so forth. Patterns of race, gender and class bias in cautioning are one result (Reiner 1995).

Further, do we want the police to build stronger cases (so that fewer innocent people suffer the stresses of prosecution and risk of miscarriages of justice)? Or do we want them not to think in terms of building cases at all but rather to think of assembling evidence (to counteract their adversarial tendency to construct evidence pointing in one direction alone)?

Giving more power to the CPS would be no solution to any of these difficulties, for - as we have seen - the CPS is as committed to successful prosecution as are the police. It is possible to conceive of some sort of 'juge d'instruction' to adjudicate on the evidence produced by the police and to order (or perhaps carry out) re-investigation where it considered it desirable (as advocated by Devlin, 1979), but:

a.   grafting inquisitorial bodies onto an adversarial system is unlikely to work;

b.   without information from non-police sources it would simply be a re-named CPS;

c.   genuine independence would require powers and resources to (re)investigate and so forth, making it likely to be reserved for serious cases only, as in France.

Germany actually abolished its equivalent of juges d'instruction for reasons on these lines. Both in France and Germany the relatively powerful prosecutors who are supposedly inquisitorial and neutral find their dual role impossible in practice (Leigh and Zedner, 1992). There are also major knock-on effects from such systems, such as delay, lengthy pre-trial detention, and so forth.

On the assumption that we keep the adversarial system, the only viable accountability for prosecution decisions is to the court. Making this a reality requires an institution prepared -and resourced - to bring everything possible to the court's attention. This means that defence lawyers need to adopt an ideology and the means of defence, which they often do not have at present (McConville *et al* 1991, Ch.8; McConville *et al* 1992). This would entail the more ready provision of criminal legal aid in general and, for defence investigation, the opening of police files to defence lawyers. It would also require more willingness to allow the defence to commission their own scientific reports where appropriate. Neither the police nor the CPS should be expected to protect the interests of the defendant.

Certain dilemmas will always remain difficult to resolve. We have seen that the interests of defendant, victim, police and state may diverge. To whom, then, should the police be accountable for prosecution decisions? To the victim (through the community)? Or to the defendant (through court insistence on due process)? Notions of 'quality of service' usually imply the former, but legal principles the latter. However, there are special cases, where application of general principles is especially difficult: sensitive issues such as sexual offences, domestic violence, racial attacks, crimes of violence and dishonesty by police officers.

Whatever the substantive policies to be pursued on such difficult issues, there is currently no coherent policy-making structure. Reform could take one of the following forms. First, the Code for Crown Prosecutors could be expanded to provide a public set of national criteria to be applied consistently across the nation. Alternatively, police authorities (or whatever local bodies replace them) could work out policies for local implementation. This would have been one of the functions of each local Police and Prosecution Authority had this proposal (for locally accountable Crown Prosecutors) of the Royal Commission on Criminal Procedure ever been implemented.

General Control Mechanisms

A number of control or accountability mechanisms applying to various areas of policing have already been discussed:

1. *Recording (manually, aurally or visually):*

   These can be evaded and/or misrepresent the nature of the encounter, for what is recorded may not be the product of an independent party, nor a joint product, but the product of one side of the encounter.

2. *Supervision:*

   It is difficult to supervise meaningfully low visibility work, so this usually amounts to supervision of police accounts of encounters (forms, written evidence, etc).

3. *Access to Legal Advice:*

   This is often evaded and of dubious value in many cases even when sought and provided before interrogation.

4. *Court control:*

   This is currently rarely meaningful. Exclusionary and corroboration rules, though, would exert some control and create more accountability to the law. An essential pre-requisite for accountability to law is that there are legal consequences for breach of it. Currently few breaches of the law by police (eg. denial of access, breach of interrogation rules, wrongful stop-search) have legal consequences (Sanders, 1988b). Legal consequences could additionally include civil compensation as well as exclusion of evidence.

5. *Police Complaints and Discipline*:

Athough a complex subject the basic problems with the current system (even since the creation of the Police Complaints Authority (PCA) in 1985) are well known:

● many complaints are not made in the first place and many others are withdrawn, due in part to pressure from the police;

● very few complaints succeed, which has worried the PCA and its predecessor (the PCB) as well as other commentators;

● investigation is done by the police themselves, providing the opportunity for discrediting complainants and partial inquiry. The PCB once commented that 'it would be helpful if ... conclusions were not preconceived but the result of the investigation.' (PCB, 1980);

● only in the most serious cases are the PCA involved in investigation, and even then they only supervise (rather than investigate themselves). Thus the PCA only rarely disagrees with the police and is in a similar position to the CPS - evaluating police work on the basis of paper work produced by the police themselves. Hence it is seen by complainants as 'on the side of the police' (Maguire and Corbett, 1991);

● hearings are not open, the documentation is secret, and the complainant has no *locus standi*. The system is a disciplinary system rather than one of redress or accountability. Thus only offences against discipline are dealt with rather than, for instance, general unfairness. And the standard of proof required is that of 'beyond reasonable doubt', which is almost unheard of outside the criminal courts.

The complaints system thus fails all due process tests, hence fails to curb the crime control orientation of the police, and thus fails to hold the police accountable to the law or to any agreed policies. As Maguire (1992) notes, it is not that investigators wish to exonerate officers who 'overstep the mark', but that policing norms create 'codes of silence' which are almost impossible to penetrate, and that 'the mark' is not a clear or unchanging line. It depends more on police culture and informal working rules than it does on the law or official policy. Thus the complaints system will be unreformable until police culture and working rules are fundamentally changed, which is not at all likely in the short or medium term.

It is interesting to see the Home Office pressing for the system to allow dismissal of incompetent or inefficient officers where proof of a disciplinary offence would be difficult. If this were done, inefficiency and incompetence could, in theory, become grounds for dismissal in cases of consistent failure to implement agreed policies or where there was persistent bias, but it is likely that rather narrower 'performance indicators' are in mind. Insofar as these could be arrest/prosecution figures this could be a retrograde step (see Maguire and Norris, 1992, on such performance indicators).

Conclusion

Several fundamental propositions about the control of discretion emerge from this discussion:

First, we should not impose rules on the police which obstruct their role, crime control, and (except sometimes in initial investigation) their adversarial stance. Controls which attempt to deny their role are of limited effectiveness.

Second, we cannot control low visibility policing except minimally and we should not try to achieve the impossible.

Third, accountability through paperwork and recording (eg. tapes, written records, CPS, PCA) is of limited effectiveness since the paperwork is a product of the officers who are supposed to be controlled by it. On the other hand, the recording of reasons for decisions in other quasi-judicial fora (eg. the Parole Board) is becoming more common and is thought properly to direct the minds of decision makers at least to some extent. Recording and written records should therefore be retained but only as a basic minimum control, not as a substitute for independent controls.

Fourth, self-policing is of limited effectiveness: the police will not always inhibit their own crime control activities. Defence lawyers and complaints investigators should be there to defend and protect while the job of the police and CPS should be to police and to prosecute.

Finally, performance indicators can influence performance as much as they monitor it. Thus, using arrest, charge and convictions as indicators will accentuate the current adversarialism of the police and the problems identified therein.

Much police reform in the recent past has been aspirational in quality with as many duties and restrictions as possible placed on police officers and prosecutors. No-one really expects 'objective' reasoning on the part of the police in difficult stop and arrest decisions, nor for the police to stop 'informal' chats whilst they can benefit from them. No-one really expects a prosecution agency to act in the interests of the defendants who are their adversaries. None of this is to say that police officers and prosecutors routinely ignore or break the rules which are designed to make them accountable. Far from it. In most cases most police officers and prosecutors behave entirely properly; but accountability is not designed to deal with the unproblematic majority of cases. It is designed to deal with the minority of cases where difficulties create pressures to behave improperly.

The fact that aspirational reform policies fail to deal with such cases does not mean that aspirational rules and standards have no effect at all. Two different arguments can be made. The first is that some officers will be more inclined to police in 'due process' ways than others. The existence of 'due process' rules, however unenforceable

they may be, gives such officers 'best practice' standards to work to
and a basis for resisting pressures to police in more coercive ways.
Abolishing unenforceable rules would, according to this argument,
weaken the position of these officers and marginalise (yet further)
their policing style.

The second argument is that rules which are only variably adhered
to lessen respect for legal rules on the part of citizens as well as
police officers, with wide ranging ripple effects. Thus, legalistic
officers can be marginalised and might find promotion difficult. The
existence of these rules and institutions creates an illusion of
fairness, yet the further ahead of reality that rules get the less
seriously the police take them. What would be, from the point of
view of the police, an imbalance of power, justifies their rule
breaking to restore a balance. The 'right of silence', for instance,
can be, as we have seen, empty for many defendants. Yet it is used
by the police to justify long detention and intimidatory interrogation
tactics.

Insofar as this second argument is valid, control ends up being
doubly thwarted: restrictions on the police and the rights of suspects
do not have their desired effects; and other rights are compromised
as a 'quid pro quo' for the supposed restrictions imposed on the
police by provisions which are in fact ineffective measures. Control
would be better achieved by abandoning aspirational controls and
strengthening viable ones. We need to make as much policing as
highly visible as possible, and then seek to control only that which
is controllable (ie. that which will not be driven underground again).
These new or reinforced controls would be traded off against the
abolition or weakening of ineffective and unenforceable controls. So
we should ensure,

a.   that rules and controls which depend on the police for their
     enforcement go with the grain of policing; whilst

b.   rules and controls which attempt to impose due process are
     enforced by other agencies; and

c) insofar as this drives certain policing 'underground' the police should derive no benefit from this.

On this basis a number of specific changes would be desirable:

1. Vague manipulable offences should be redefined. The latter include public order offences where there need be no evidence that anyone felt threatened, and offensive weapon offences where suspects find it difficult to show that articles such as work tools are being carried for legitimate reasons.

2. Powers of stop and search should be abolished, but arrest should be allowed where there is 'honest' or 'genuine' suspicion. The 'reasonable grounds' requirement would be abandoned but arrest on a random or malicious basis would, of course, still be unlawful. There would be little practical change brought about by the change to arrest powers (as 'unreasonable' suspicion is currently so hard to prove), but it would bring the law into line with reality and encourage officers to report their actions and suspicions honestly. Abolition of stop and search powers would balance the widening of arrest powers and restrict interference with liberty on the street. The combined effect would be to encourage more police interrogation in the station and less on the street, making evidence-gathering (particularly through interrogation) more visible and more susceptible to control.

3. Detention following arrest and prior to charge should be made automatic but reduced to very few hours. The first suggestion would bring the law into line with practice and the second would enhance the protection of the suspect, counter-balancing the enhanced arrest powers suggested above. Further detention would be possible only if authorised by a court, with legal representation, and only if very strict criteria were met (as required now for detention beyond 36 hours).

4. Legal representation should be automatic when in custody unless it is positively refused by the suspect. Interrogation should be allowed only before a legal advisor and/or magistrate. Thus,

where the police are adversarial they should not be made self-accountable; instead, defendants should be accorded the rights they need to ensure that the police really are accountable to the law. As a vital part of this there should be more extensive legal and financial resources for defence lawyers (as detailed above) for, all too often, they currently fail their clients badly.

5. The products of informal interviewing should be inadmissible. Informal interviewing has re-introduced 'verballing', which is precisely what the elaborate arrangements in PACE for formal interviewing, tape recording and so forth were supposed to eradicate. All other evidence obtained following a breach of PACE and the Codes (including the provisions for tape recording and written records) should also be inadmissible in view of the ineffectiveness of the complaints system in controlling such breaches.

6. Consideration should be given to putting the onus in relation to intent on the defendant. Thus the police would only need to interrogate to secure evidence of intent to commit the crime in question if the circumstances created significant doubt about the presence of intent. Although this might place pressure on suspects to talk to the police in police stations it would change the emphasis from the police trying to construct their case (as now) to the suspect constructing theirs, returning some control to suspects. Insofar as this would compromise the right of silence it would do so no more than is produced by current pressures.

7. Constabulary independence should be abolished. This is a historical anachronism dating from a period in history when it was perceived as a necessary protection against local or central State interference. It now simply serves as a barrier to effective supervision and control. The effect would be to make police forces per se responsible for decisions to prosecute or not and thus put more onus on chief constables and the bodies to which they are accountable to devise and monitor non-discriminatory arrest, charge, and prosecution policies. In relation to prosecutions, the CPS could act as some kind of protection for

individual officers and victims who are dissatisfied with any decisions they believe to have been improperly imposed. The CPS itself should be controlled more tightly through publicly debated and publicised policies, devised either locally or nationally.

8. The police should be allowed to charge on whatever basis they want (subject to the kind of policy canvassed in 7. above) and the defence should be given the resources they need to challenge and defend those charges. The money for this would come from reduced spending on the CPS (it no longer having to do the defence's job of reviewing cases to see if they should be prosecuted) and fewer prosecutions, as the prospect of vigorous well-resourced adversarial defence lawyers should lead to fewer weak cases being prosecuted. As part of this there should be a corroboration rule preventing conviction on the basis of confession evidence alone, thus requiring the police to investigate more fully (McConville 1993). Only magistrates should be allowed to make formal caution (as distinct from prosecution) decisions in order that the diversion system be rescued from the abuses to which it is sometimes currently subjected. All these proposals flow from an enhancement of the adversarial principles which are supposed to structure the criminal justice system.

9. Complaints against the police should be investigated by a genuinely independent body (with police secondees), with a new emphasis on eliminating bias and discrimination. Less weight should be given to formalities of evidence, proof and punishment except in relation to very serious allegations. A 'community policing'-style investigation, adjudication and resolution process is needed. The conciliation element of some PACE complaints procedures are a sign of what can be done in this respect and this element should be built upon.

It should not be thought that, even if implemented in full, these recommended changes would eradicate miscarriages of justice or secure full police accountability. The police are like many other professionals: we must allow them to exercise their judgement in order to fulfil their role and it is impossible to control entirely that exercise of judgement. Where the police do differ from other professionals is in their adversarial relationship with the suspect, and it is for this reason that as much control as is practically possible is needed.

Note

1.   Police and Criminal Evidence Act, (PACE) SS. 1, 24, 25.

Bibliography

Baldwin J and Bedward J (1991) 'Summarising tape recordings of police interviewing', *Criminal Law Review*, p.671.

Black D (1970) 'Production of crime rates', *American Sociological Review*, 35:733.

Devlin P (1979) *The Judge*, Oxford University Press, Oxford.

Dixon D, Bottomley A, Coleman C, Gill M and Wall D (1989) 'Reality and rules in the construction and regulation of police suspicion', *International Journal of the Sociology of Law*, 17:185.

Dixon D, Bottomley A, Coleman C, Gill M and Wall D (1990a) 'Safeguarding the rights of suspects in Police custody', *Policing And Society*, 1:115.

Dixon D, Coleman C and Bottomley A (1990b) 'Consent and the legal regulation of policing', *Journal Of Law And Society*, 17:345.

Evans R (1993) *The Conduct of Police Interviews With Juveniles*, (RCCJ), HMSO, London.

Evans R and Ferguson T (1991) *Comparing Different Juvenile Cautioning Systems in one Police Force*, Home Office, London. (unpublished).

Gudjonssen G and MacKeith J (1982) 'False confessions', in Trankell A, ed. *Reconstructing the Past*, Deventer, Netherlands.

Holdaway S (1983) *Inside the British Police*, Blackwells, Oxford.

Irving B and McKenzie I (1989) *Police Interrogation: The Effects of the PACE Act*, Police Foundation, London.

Jefferson T and Walker M (1992) 'Ethnic minorities in the criminal justice system', *Criminal Law Review*, p.83.

Kay T (1991) *Unsafe And Unsatisfactory*, Cobden Trust, London.

Leigh L and Zedner L (1992) *Report on the Administration of Criminal Justice in France and Germany* (RCCJ) HMSO, London.

Lustgarten L,(1987) 'The police and the substantive criminal law', *British Journal Of Criminology*, 27:23.

Maguire M and Corbett C (1991) *A Study Of The Police Complaints System*, HMSO, London.

Maguire M and Norris C (1992) *The Conduct and Supervision of Criminal Investigations*, (RCCJ). HMSO, London.

Maguire M (1992) 'Complaints against the police: Where now?', (unpublished paper).

Matza D (1969), *Becoming Deviant*, Prentice Hall, New Jersey.

McConville M and Morrel P (1983) 'Recording and interrogation: Have the police got it taped?', *Criminal Law Review*, p.158.

McConville M, Sanders A and Leng R (1991) *Courts, Prosecution and Conviction*, Oxford University Press, Oxford.

McConville M, Sanders A and Leng R (1991) *The Case For The Prosecution*, Routledge, London.

McConville M and Hodgson J (1992) *Custodial Legal Advice and the Right to Silence*, (RCCJ) HMSO, London.

McConville M (1992) 'Videotaping Interrogations: Police behaviour on and off camera', *Criminal Law Review*, p.52.

McConville M (1993) 'The effect of a corroboration rule', (RCCJ) HMSO, London.

McKenzie I, Morgan R and Reiner R (1990) 'Helping the police with their enquiries', *Criminal Law Review*, p.22.

Police Complaints Board (1980), *Triennial Report*, HMSO, London.

Reiner R (1985) *The Politics of the Police*, Harvest-Wheatsheaf, Brighton.

Sanders A (1985) 'Prosecution decisions and the Attorney-General guidelines', *Criminal Law Review*, p.4.

Sanders A (1988a) 'Personal violence and public order: The prosecution of domestic violence in England and Wales', *International Journal of Sociology of Law*, 16:359.

Sanders A (1988b) 'Rights, remedies and the PACE Act', *Criminal Law Review*, p.802.

Sanders A, Bridges L, Mulvaney A and Crozier G (1989) *Advice and Assistance at Police Stations and the 24 Hour Duty Solicitor Scheme*, LCD, London.

Sanders A and Bridges L (1990) 'Access to legal advice', in C Walker and K Sturmer (ed), *Justice in Error*, Blackstone, London.

Scarman L (1981) *The Scarman Report: The Brixton Disorders*, HMSO, London.

Smith D and Gray J (1983) *Police and People in London*, PSI, London.

Steer D (1980) *Uncovering Crime: The Police Role*, HMSO, London.

Stone C (1989) *Public Interest Case Assessment*, (VERA, New York).

Willis C (1983) *The Use, Effectiveness and Impact of Police Stop and Search Powers*, Home Office, RPV Paper 15, London.

5. THE INTERNATIONAL DIMENSION
Neil Walker

In the present chapter we look beyond the purely domestic context to consider UK involvement in the developing field of international policing. This switch of focus demands certain alterations to the approach adopted in previous chapters, two of which are particularly salient. In the first place, whereas in the purely domestic arena we encounter deeply entrenched institutions and practices and must to some extent work with the grain of this tradition when engaged in evaluation and advocating reform, existing arrangements weigh rather less heavily when we come to assess policy options in the international context. In this more fluid and rapidly evolving area of activity the answers provided to broad questions of public policy concerning the general direction and scope of policing activity remain highly provisional and open to fundamental review. Secondly, as we shall see, the relationship between the legitimacy and effectiveness of police activity may be significantly different in the international context than in the domestic context, and this must be taken into account when addressing questions of institutional (re)design.

Despite these differences, however, there are compelling empirical and normative grounds for treating our investigation of decision-making in international policing as basically continuous with our more general analysis of the domestic scene. Empirically, the two spheres of activity are closely related; Domestic arrangements exert a considerable influence over international developments, and vice-versa. Normatively, although the different working environment and audiences of international policing caution against the unreflective transcription of ideas and mechanisms of good practice from the domestic context, the underlying standard of assessment and aspiration guiding inquiry remains the same, namely, a set of policing arrangements which is satisfactory in terms of both effectiveness and accountability.

Before we engage in this key evaluative stage of our investigation, we must lay the necessary foundations. First, we set out the present position in the UK in respect of international police co-operation. Thereafter, we look beneath the surface to investigate the political dynamic which drives development in this area. By focussing on the pattern of underlying interests and the strategic context within which present trends are unfolding, this analysis helps us to assess how far removed is the evolving structure from the ideal and what obstacles stand in the way of reform.

The Present Position

Political justifications for increased international police co-operation are marked by their diversity and by their appeal to broad propositions whose evidential basis is unclear but which, equally, are difficult to falsify. The most general and most longstanding line of argument emphasises the broad trend towards greater mobility of the individual criminal and an increase in the international dimension of criminal networks and transactions; in particular, the significant growth since the 1970s in serious international crimes such as terrorism, drug-trafficking and money laundering is highlighted (Home Affairs Committee, 1991, v-vi). A more recent and rather more focused argument is that the abolition or, at the very least, substantial relaxation of internal border controls between EC Member States in accordance with the '1992' single market programme will destroy the traditional filter function of frontiers and so remove a considerable physical and psychological impediment to international crime. A final major theme, of yet more recent vintage, also centres on the EC but is concerned with the security of its outer shell rather than its internal compartments (Latter, 1991). This argument points to the difficulties of stemming the migratory flow from poor regions in the South and East which has been encouraged by major geo-political developments. It emphasises the consequent danger of an exponential development of clandestine immigration and unsubstantiated asylum claims, and the need for compensatory developments in law enforcement co-operation (Den Boer and Walker, 1993).

We shall return to the merits of these arguments and their implications for future developments at a later point. For the moment we may note that the division between the specifically EC dimension and the wider international dimension is mirrored in the range of institutional arrangements for transnational co-operation in which the UK has become involved. In recent years, consistent with the broader economic and political transformation of the EC since the UK obtained membership in 1972, it is the first of these dimensions which has gradually come to provide the single most important institutional focus for police co-operation. However, activity in a diversity of other international contexts, old and new, remains at a significant level. It is noteworthy that the overall profile of British involvement in international policing does not reveal a single integrated pattern, but rather an opaque patchwork of agencies and initiatives with distinct but overlapping institutional sources, territorial remits, functional specialisms and strategic emphases.

Trevi

If, therefore, we begin with the EC as the most prominent sector, the anchor of international policing efforts within its territory has been the Trevi group. Set up in 1975 and originally intended as an inter-governmental platform for EC Ministers of Justice and Home Affairs to develop counter-terrorist measures, both its mandate and its organisational support have become gradually extended over the years. As presently constituted it has a three-tier structure, including a ministerial level, a senior official level, and a series of Working Groups made up of officials and police officers. Apart from the original anti-terrorism group (Trevi 1), other permanent specialist groups have been established in recent years: Trevi 2 deals with police training and technology, Trevi 3 with serious crime and public order and Trevi 4 with disaster prevention, while the policing consequences of the abolition of internal frontiers were addressed by Trevi 92 until it was disbanded in recognition of the passage of the official deadline for the completion of the internal market. Finally, alongside these permanent working groups there are various *ad hoc* groups such as that which is presently addressing the establishment of Europol and another which was set up in June 1992 following the murder of the Italian judge Giovanni Falcone in order to combat organised crime in the EC (Van Outrive, 1992b, 1992d).

Another recent indication of the expanding remit of Trevi was provided by the Action Programme agreed at the Dublin Meeting of the European Council in 1990. The areas identified for development in this new programme, which was inspired at least in part by concern over the consequences of the 1992 initiative, include exchange of liaison officers, controls at internal and external borders, a European Information System (EIS), and new communication methods, training exchanges and technical and scientific supports. More generally, the 1992 programme has encouraged greater cross-fertilisation between the activities of Trevi and other EC institutions and quasi-institutions. The Co-ordinators Group on the security implications of the free movement of persons which was set up at the Rhodes European Council in 1988 has, through its Palma document (House of Lords, 1989, 55-63), attempted to provide an integrated programme of change. Within this wider perspective, the work of Trevi is closely complemented by that of bodies such as the Mutual Assistance Group (MAG '92) which is concerned with customs co-operation, and the Ad Hoc Group on Immigration which was responsible for drafting the Dublin Convention on Asylum in 1990 and the as yet unconcluded External Frontiers Convention. It has since been instrumental in developing a work programme for the more general harmonisation of the immigration and asylum policies of Member States (HM Government, 1992, 9).

Europol

Despite acting as a short term stimulus to Trevi and its network of associated agencies, the progress of European integration threatens over the longer course to absorb many of the functions of the older body within a deeper and wider regulatory structure. The treaty of Maastricht which was signed in February 1991 establishes a new European Union which extends beyond the traditional institutions and jurisdiction of the European Communities and brings policing and criminal justice policy under its umbrella. In particular, the key provision within the Treaty (Article K.1.9) establishes an agency to be known as Europol. It thus brings to fruition an idea which, largely through the efforts of German commentators and politicians (Van Outrive, 1992a), had lurked on the margins of the European political agenda since the early 1970s until it was made the subject of a specific proposal by Chancellor Kohl to the Luxembourg European Council in June 1991. The foundation provision for Europol envisages a system of information exchange for the purposes of preventing and combating terrorism, drug-trafficking and other serious forms of international crime (Art K.1.(9)). Further, the associated Political Declaration of the Member States commits its signatories: (1) to explore ways to co-ordinate national investigation and search operations with an international dimension; (2) to create new databases; (3) to provide a central analytical facility for the planning of criminal investigations; (4) to explore supranational initiatives in respect of crime prevention; and (5) to make further collaborative progress in training, research, forensic science and criminal records.

As intimated above, while this undoubtedly marks a qualitative shift in the politics of police co-operation, it would be a mistake to view Europol and its related measures as establishing a new hegemony in this field. To begin with, the Treaty is couched in extremely general terms. Its list of general commitments allows a variety of alternative interpretations and fails to specify either a particular order of priorities or a definite schedule for progress. In particular, beyond a bland commitment in the Political Declaration to review the scope for further development by 1994, there is no attempt to address whether, still less how or when, Europol or any successor organisation might develop as a police force with full operational capacity, including powers of arrest, search and questioning.

The vagueness of the Maastricht mandate on Europol is reflected in the faltering pace of post-Maastricht progress. Despite agreement to place the establishment of a European Drugs Unit and a European Information System at the top of the agenda[1], as was acknowledged at the Edinburgh summit of the European Council in December 1992 (European Council 1992, para.24), the commitment to have a working agency in place by the end of that year eventually proved to be unrealistic. Furthermore, the fact that the failure to meet this timetable was in large part attributable to an inability to resolve even the most basic question of the location of the new organisation, provides eloquent testimony to the formidable political difficulties which must be overcome in developing the Europol organisation. To the original options of Wiesbaden, Lyons and Strasbourg, the Trevi 'Europol' sub-committee considering this issue was persuaded to add two other possibilities, namely Rome and The Hague[2], with the latter three sites still in contention after the inconclusive Trevi ministerial meeting prior to the Edinburgh summit[3].

Another area of uncertainty surrounding the new initiative concerns the relationship between Europol and the broader structure of EC institutions and quasi-institutions. The general policy area of Justice and Home Affairs is recognised for the first time within the Treaty as a separate 'pillar' of Community activity in its own right. Accordingly, Europol is embedded within a broad regulatory framework which also includes matters such as immigration, asylum and external borders policy, wider strategies to combat international fraud and drug addiction, as well as activities falling under the rubric of customs co-operation and judicial co-operation in civil and criminal matters (Art.K.1). However, although an overarching role is provided for the Council of Ministers (the political executive of the EC, Art.K.3) aided by a new Co-ordinating Committee of permanent representatives (Art.K.4), and although a generic approach to matters which are functionally related offers the theoretical prospect of a more integrated policy-making process (Boys Smith, 1992) than that which the loose networking of the Co-ordinators Group presently allows, it remains unclear how in practice traditionally discrete policy sectors will be co-ordinated with one another. Relatedly, the fate of extant Community-wide institutional structures which occupy the same policy space is not apparent from the new Treaty. In particular, while, as intimated, much of the existing Trevi apparatus will become redundant - indeed, there has already been established a new committee anticipating the role of the post-Maastricht Co-ordinating Committee of permanent representatives[4] - it is suggested in some influential quarters that the key matter of anti-terrorist co-operation will remain under the aegis of the latter group (Den Boer and Walker, 1993).

Post Maastricht

A final and most significant source of intrinsic uncertainty with regard to the new Treaty provisions concerns the very survival of the ratification process. Rejection of the Treaty in its entirety in the initial Danish referendum in May 1992, a wafer-thin majority in the French referendum in September and a more general wavering of support throughout the EC has thrown the whole project of a deeper European Union into a state of turmoil which was only partially relieved by the modest rapprochement achieved at the Edinburgh summit and by the reversal of the earlier 'no vote' in a second Danish referendum in May 1993. Even if the Maastricht initiative eventually emerges unscathed, the impact of the Eurosceptic countercurrent has been to provide a timely reminder that the tide of integration is not inexorable and that the centrality of an EC dimension in this or any other aspect of international relations remains provisional.

More immediately, the turbulent political environment alters the terms of debate concerning current developments and strengthens the hand of conservative forces. Under such circumstances, even where the legal position is clearly favourable to increased co-operation, the vulnerability of the broader project is such that there may be a reluctance to press claims on the one side, and a preparedness to re-open possibilities and pursue options previously foreclosed on the other. In consequence, as has been shown in a number of areas pertinent to our inquiries, relatively settled issues tend to re-emerge as the subject of political negotiation. One example is the European Commission's insistence that Article 8A of the EEC Treaty required the abolition of all internal frontier controls by the end of 1992 (European Commission, 1992) and its pledge to pursue or support legal action to compel recalcitrant Member States to abide by this interpretation[5]. As part of a broader strategy of self-restraint to counter expansionist fears in the changed atmosphere following the

Danish referendum result, the Commission subsequently changed
tack and sought a compromise solution with the UK which would
allow the latter to continue general spot checks of passports of intra-
EC travellers at its ports of entry[6]. In the event, a broader range of
factors combined to frustrate the implementation of the free
movement regime throughout the Community in general by the due
date (European Council, 1992, paras.17-20), but in the post-1992
climate the UK position continues to be marked by a reluctance to
make a long-term commitment to the abolition of systematic
controls, while the Commission has been careful to maintain a
non-confrontational approach[7].

Similarly, responding to the mood of deep uncertainty over the fate
of the Maastricht Treaty just prior to the French referendum, the UK
Home Secretary voiced his support for inter-governmental
co-operation on policing as a failsafe in the event of non-ratification.
He thereby re-established on the political agenda an option which
seemed in any case to have been the preferred alternative of the UK
Government in the pre-Maastricht period[8]. A retreat to inter-
governmentalism appeared to become a more likely option upon the
conclusion in October 1992 of an agreement by seven of the eight
political parties represented in the Danish Folketing to support
ratification of the Maastricht Treaty in a second referendum only if
certain conditions were met, including the provision of an option not
to participate in co-operative measures on justice and home affairs[9],
and the later intimation by the UK Conservative government, in the
face of deep ambivalence within its own party, of an intention to
delay the enactment of the Maastricht Treaty into UK law until the
second Danish referendum had been held[10].

Subsequent events at and beyond the Edinburgh summit stemmed
the drift back to inter-governmentalism at a formal institutional level
but may have offered some encouragement to political activity
geared to the same objective. On the one hand, the new Treaty
obligations of Member States in this area were not questioned, and
in the case of Denmark they were reconfirmed (European Council,
1992, Annex 1). On the other hand, an accompanying unilateral
declaration by Denmark (Annex 3) emphasised the need for

unanimity in the Council on justice and home affairs issues and introduced a domestic requirement for special voting majorities to ratify any developments in integrated policy in this field. In other words, the Danish government sought to emphasise the scope for *de facto* inter-governmentalism within the legal framework of the new Chapter, a point which will not have been lost on other governments, including the UK government, which are ambivalent about the rate and direction of progress.

Outwith the EC

As suggested earlier, the EC dimension remains in any event only one of a number of spheres of active influence within international police and criminal justice co-operation in which UK interests participate or by which they are affected. Indeed, there is arguably a pattern of mutual causality here. It seems both that the prior existence of various alternative avenues for co-operation exacerbates uncertainties about the development of Europol and associated EC initiatives, and that the weaknesses in the new EC structures already diagnosed offer encouragement and political space for additional growth by non-EC agencies.

For example, traditional fora pitched at a level wider than the EC, such as Interpol and the Council of Europe, have extended and deepened their impact in recent years. As the oldest and largest inter-governmental organisation in the area of police co-operation, Interpol provides the major communications network for the passage of criminal intelligence and other messages and requests between national police authorities. It has recently enhanced its image and operational capacity in the European context through the creation of a European Secretariat and Technical Committee together with the initiation of a European Liaison Bureau at Lyons and a contact officer network covering the National Central Bureaux of the European members (Walker, 1991, 28-31; Kendall, 1992). For its part, in the European context the Council of Europe has traditionally provided the most fertile source of international legislative initiatives in the broad field of criminal justice co-operation. To an older series of Treaties which pursued a repressive strategy, including measures on extradition (1957), mutual legal assistance (1959), validity of judgements (1970) and transfer of proceedings (1972), there has recently been added a new crop which encapsulate a more preventative philosophy, including measures on the suppression of terrorism (1988), insider trading (1989) and money laundering (1990). While the UK government was slow to embrace many of the older Treaties, the key extradition and mutual legal assistance agreements not receiving ratification until 1990, it has been notably more enthusiastic over the second wave: for example, the Suppression of Terrorism Convention was ratified in the year following its signature, while in September 1992 the UK was the first signatory state to ratify the new Money Laundering Convention (Hondius, 1992).

Further, other institutions whose jurisdiction extends beyond the EC have emerged as significant players in the domain of police and criminal justice co-operation in recent years. The United Nations itself, for example, was responsible for a major breakthrough in the co-ordination of international policy against drug-trafficking when, in Vienna in December 1988, it concluded its Convention against Illicit Traffic in Narcotic Drugs and Psychotropic Substances. Further, an entirely new agency known as the Financial Action Task Force has recently been active in a similar area. Having been established by the Heads of State of the seven leading industrialised nations (Group of Seven) meeting together with the President of the European Commission in July 1989, it has quickly developed a wide-ranging policy programme to counter the laundering of drug funds (Gilmore, 1992, xviii-xix).

Even within its own region, moreover, the hegemony of the EC in police co-operation matters is not assured. A direct challenge is posed by the Schengen Agreements of 1985 and 1990 (Den Boer, 1991a), to which the UK is not a signatory. These have set out to establish a border-free zone, together with compensatory initiatives in the areas of police and judicial co-operation, sealing of external borders etc, between those Member States, (increased from an original core of five and presently numbering nine) who have sought to anticipate progress under the single market programme. Although there have subsequently been unforeseen delays in the implementation of this initiative, with only four states having completed the ratification process so far, this, paradoxically, has served to heighten rather than diminish the uncertainty surrounding the rival Europol initiative. This is so because many of the obstacles to progress under Schengen, including controversies over the scope and security of the Schengen Information System and the use of operational police powers by officers outwith their national jurisdiction, are likely to provide just as obstinate stumbling blocks in the development of Europol.

In any event, despite its tentative progress, the Schengen initiative remains decidedly more advanced than Europol. Accordingly, while it is sometimes assumed from the similarity of their proposed mandates that Schengen, as the territorially more restricted organisation, will eventually be absorbed into the larger Europol, the recent revival of proposals for a 'multi-tier' (Federal Trust, 1991), or two-speed Europe in the light of continuing uncertainty over the ratification of Maastricht may encourage an inner core to press ahead with Schengen as a long-term institutional settlement rather than as a mere stepping stone to a wider agreement[11].

Just as the idea of a Europol dedicated to the current EC Member States faces competition on the inside lane, so too it is challenged on the outside lane by those within its strategic planning circles who would like the remit of the putative Europol to be expanded. Its initial terms of reference address the prospect of co-operation between members and non-members of the EC (Boys Smith, 1992) and there is continuing support for the inclusion of Austria, Switzerland and the countries of Eastern Europe together with the core Twelve as full members of the new organisation (Van Outrive, 1992a). Indeed, rather than acting as a rival alternative, the expanded Europol option might plausibly be seen as complementing Schengen within a two-speed Europe, as the other claw in a pincer which would cut off the development of Europol as currently envisaged.

Finally, it should be noted that developments and proposals at the multilateral or supranational level associated with the well-established international organisations must also run alongside a range of more modest initiatives which exhibit a greater or lesser degree of formality. In the case of the UK, there are, towards the formal end of the continuum, two significant bilateral agreements. First, there is the Anglo-Irish Agreement, with its comparatively modest provision for joint threat assessment, exchange of information and technical knowledge, training, operations planning etc. (Home Affairs Committee, 1990, xv). Secondly, further to the Channel Fixed Link Treaty, many of the arrangements necessary for the policing of the channel tunnel, which is to be operational by 1994, have been put in place. Under the Channel Tunnel Act 1987, the Chief Constable of Kent has been made responsible for the policing of the tunnel at the English end. More generally, under the Policing and Frontiers Control Protocol to the Fixed Link Treaty provision is made for mutual assistance and co-ordination between the UK and French border forces in respect of frontier controls, prevention and detection of crime and public safety measures, as well as for the establishment of permanent communication links, liaison officers and joint strategy meetings (Harding, 1991). In turn, a complementary set of organisational reforms within the Kent Police, and in particular the development of a new, multi-functional Frontier Controls Unit reflects and encourages a broader pattern of cross-channel liaison and intercourse between operational officers.

Other examples towards the more informal end of the continuum include initiatives and practices in policy making and operational circles, at both local and national levels, within and outwith mainstream policing. For senior police officers, the International Association of Chiefs of Police which in recent years has extended its activities from its American base and developed an active European Branch, and the annual conference of Heads of Police Forces of European Capital Cities, provide fora for general discussion of policy matters. More modestly, senior officers in five English forces are involved in a continuing dialogue with Dutch, Belgian and French colleagues in the longstanding Cross-Channel Intelligence Conference. Further, HM Customs and Excise, which also has a key international policing role in terms of its responsibility to control the movement of goods liable to duty or forfeiture, and the people carrying them, through UK ports and airports, is involved in a separate set of international policy networks. Alongside the MAG '92 Group mentioned earlier, there is also the global Customs Co-operation Council based in Brussels.

If we move to the operational level, individual forces, through specialist agencies such as drugs, fraud and serious crime squads each develop their own networks of informal contacts and the same is true of the Regional Crime Squads. At the national level, the European Liaison Section of the Metropolitan Police Special Branch has acted as an important medium for international liaison on anti-terrorist matters. The National Criminal Intelligence Service (NCIS), newly established in April 1992, provides an unprecedented focal point for the development of international working relations in crime matters more generally, although its particular strength still lies with its Drugs Division which has succeeded the National Drugs Intelligence Unit. Finally, other national operational bodies whose remit allows for the development of international liaison include the Serious Fraud office, the British Transport Police, the Investigation Division of HM Customs and Excise and the Immigration Service (Walker, 1991, 31-37)

The Political Dynamic of International Police Co-operation

General Trends

It is apparent, therefore, that the domain of international police co-operation may aptly be depicted as a 'crowded policy space' (Raab, 1992). Agencies with different mandates, political allegiances, philosophies of police co-operation, projections of social and political developments and vested interests co-exist in relationships which at best amount to *ad hoc* mutual aid and accommodation and at worse descend into open competition over scarce economic and symbolic resources (Van Reenen, 1989; Bigo, 1992). Accordingly, even with the advent of Europol, there is at present no strong institutional momentum in favour of any particular overall settlement. If, however, we move beyond this general description of the current pattern of arrangements, can we discern any more specific underlying dynamic guiding reform ?

We may begin by noting that, just as in the domestic domain, any analysis of police development must be careful not to attach too much store by the independent causal significance of environmental factors (Grimshaw and Jefferson, 1987, 9-11), this is equally, if not more the case in the international domain. Put bluntly, the development of international policing in any particular direction is in no sense compelled by or even strongly influenced by the demands of international crime and security. This is true not only in the obvious sense that there is never an objectively ascertainable optimal response to any particular profile of deviant activity within or across communities - for the simple reason that it is logically impossible to derive an institutional 'ought' from an environmental 'is' - but also in the sense that what constitutes the 'problem' of international crime and security is itself in many respects highly controversial.

There are a number of aspects to this argument. To begin with, the *absolute* level of, or threat, of international crime remains deeply obscure. Drug-trafficking, money laundering and other international frauds, for example, typically take place in regions of low visibility where the 'dark figure' of crime remains stubbornly in the shadows. Other recent growth areas such as international auto theft and art and antiquities theft suffer from the same measurement problem (Gregory and Collier, 1991). Terrorism, by its nature, is a more visible phenomenon, but because of the understandable investment in pre-emptive strategies in this field, it is unclear what the potential dimensions of the problem are and what, therefore, is required by way of policing to contain it within certain levels.

A second argument points to the *relative seriousness* with which many international crimes are viewed. Any purely quantifiable analysis of the crime problem is always unsatisfactory to the extent that it purports to compare incommensurables. However, this is particularly so with crimes such as terrorism and drug-trafficking which pose such a profound threat to the state and civil society respectively that many would argue that they defy meaningful comparison with most 'normal' crimes.

Thirdly, there is the question of *overall trends*. In particular, if we focus on the significance of the 1992 programme, it remains highly controversial just what impact the removal of border controls has had and will have on the incidence of international crime. Some, including the British police, would argue that borders, in particular sea borders, provide 'the first opportunity for prevention and the last chance of detection' (Home Affairs Committee, 1992, 95) and that their lifting removes important physical and psychological barriers to international crime. Others argue that they have little effect and that the detection and preventive work presently carried out at borders could be done just as effectively elsewhere (Latter, 1991). As both arguments tend to rely upon counterfactuals and upon evidence open to competing interpretations, this issue remains a key imponderable in the overall debate.

Finally, there is a fundamental *discursive* problem. Should the issues which tend to be addressed in predominantly law enforcement terms be viewed through such a conceptual grid at all? Again, this is a pervasive problem in the evaluation of policing and we should be careful not to overstate the difficulty by creating a false dichotomy. Thus, for example, that drug abuse and terrorism have social and political roots which may be amenable to treatment given the requisite political will does not mean that it is inappropriate to acknowledge a law enforcement dimension to these problems, although questions of priority will remain controversial.

While these are deeply embedded problems with equally deeply rooted institutional responses, there are, however, other emergent problems within the international agenda whose fundamental categorisation is open to dispute but which are already tending to be subsumed under a law and order discourse. As intimated earlier, the question of asylum and immigration policy within the EC is one such issue. As has been powerfully argued by the French commentator, Didier Bigo, the constant association of a variety of different themes in the language and practice of European politicians has created a mutually reinforcive 'internal security ideology', with each substantive topic across a broad spectrum presented as but one component of an indivisible 'security deficit' in the new Europe *sans frontieres* (Bigo, 1992). Thus, rather than being seen as a complex humanitarian problem brought about by migrants from economically dispossessed, socially unstable or politically oppressed parts of the world coming up against the 'hard outer core' of a prosperous Community reluctant to dilute its riches by sharing them too widely, the increased pressure within immigration and asylum channels is viewed more narrowly as a matter which must in large part be resolved through a policy of exclusion, if only to compensate for the various other criminogenic developments in international relations. Underlining Bigo's analysis, this terse assessment of the operation of the new European 'internal security field' was recently offered by a Committee of the European Parliament:

> 'the same standard list - crime, terrorism, drugs policy, illegal aliens and asylum-seekers - is always reeled off by those wishing to emphasise the importance of co-operation between police forces. This populist approach and lack of dispassionateness [sic] are regrettable' (Van Outrive, 1992c, 19).

It is clear, therefore, that the problems of international crime are in no sense self-evident. Rather than a verifiable assessment of the extent and seriousness of the overall threat which provides a clear pointer to preventive and repressive strategies, what is instead available is a highly ambiguous set of messages. If the field of international law enforcement constitutes a crowded policy space, it is at least in part because the discursive space which it occupies is, by contrast, so liberally defined. As Bigo points out, it is a field of argument and practice in which the pursuit and justification of a broad range of different security philosophies, and indeed of wider political agendas, are capable of being dressed up in the emotive but persuasive rhetoric of 'law and order'. If this is the case what, then, are the wider policy undercurrents which direct the agenda of police co-operation in the UK ?

The UK's International Agenda

In line with the institutional bifurcation discussed earlier, the key political debate over the pace and direction of development tends to revolve around whether and to what extent the Europol/EC route should be followed. To begin with, we may note that there are both general and particular reasons for UK reluctance to be in the integrationist vanguard. Generally, there is broad ambivalence in the UK position towards *soi disant* federalist developments in Europe. The UK's reputation as 'an awkward partner' (George, 1990) in the Community venture dates from its accession in 1972. Today there remain significant oppositional forces in both major parties (Bulpitt, 1992; Tindale, 1992), the spectre of whose alliance has recently haunted both a Government committed to the legislative endorsement of the Maastricht Treaty and an Opposition concerned to project a united pro-European front. In turn, given that the nation state has traditionally been defined in terms of its control of the means of internal and external violence within a territory (Jessop, 1991, 343) and, therefore, that its integrity is commonly perceived as intimately dependent upon its control and successful execution of a policing function, it is unsurprising that this function remains a jealously protected domestic prerogative in a political culture which remains dedicated to the preservation of a large measure of national sovereignty[12].

More specifically, within EC political discourse, as we have seen, the whole issue of police co-operation has become bound up with the question of open internal borders. Indeed in the official policy of the European Commission (European Commission, 1988, para. 16(vii)) co-operation is viewed as one means of compensating for the security deficit flowing from a régime of free movement. As a persistent opponent of an open frontiers policy on the grounds of the disproportionate security implications of the loss of sea borders, the UK's position on police co-operation has been somewhat compromised by its stance on that prior question of principle. Further, some of the more specific *actions compensatoires* which have been mooted, including compulsory ID cards, the introduction of registration schemes in camp sites and hotels throughout the

Community and the imposition of punitive sanctions on the employers of unauthorised workers, would require more significant adjustment of the boundaries of privacy and legitimate police action in the UK than in many other Member States (Latter, 1991, 5-6; Lyon, 1991; Owers, 1992)[13].

Nevertheless, the UK Government has a strong interest in effective co-operation in certain key areas of international crime. As the territorial base of the largest and most resilient terrorist movement in the EC, the UK government has traditionally been at the forefront of international anti-terrorist measures, as shown by its leading role in the establishment of Trevi in 1976 and of the Police Working Group on Terrorism in 1979 and in its early ratification of the 1977 Council of Europe Convention on the Suppression of Terrorism (Riley, 1991). Similarly, in the area of drug-trafficking and associated money laundering activities, as a leading international financial centre the UK has been a significant focus of activity (Wren, 1992). It has been in the vanguard of recent efforts to develop practical means of assistance both at the legal level, in its strong support for recent United Nations, Council of Europe and EC initiatives, and at the institutional level, through its proposal of a European Drugs Intelligence Unit (an early blueprint for the European Drugs Unit and for Europol itself) in 1989 (Walker, 1991).

More generally, UK governments and professional élites have traditionally involved themselves in international co-operation over a broader range of crimes and practical policing problems and so have tended to encourage a flexible range of developments. As was apparent from our earlier discussion, these have been by no means restricted to the territorial boundaries or formal institutional avenues of the EC. For example, the Foreign and Commonwealth Office has recently been active in sending British police advisory teams to the fledgling democracies of Eastern Europe, including Poland and the (former) Czech and Slovak Federal Republic (Gregory, 1992). There is a more longstanding tradition of UK influence in training, organisational and technical matters in various Asian and African states. Indeed, further underlining their influence in circumstances of political transition, UK officers have been involved in a monitoring and advisory role in respect of the problems of discipline, morale and legitimacy currently affecting the South African police as they adjust to a changing balance of social and political power; for example, following allegations of police involvement in the Boipatong massacre in June 1992 the Goldstone Commission which was charged with its investigation asked two senior officers from Scotland Yard to audit the effectiveness of its own performance[14].

Likewise, even where the UK restricts its activities to the EC, co-operation is broadly based and by no means confined to the most topical and most immediately pressing subjects of co-operation. The commitment of the UK government during its presidency of Trevi in the latter half of 1992 to promote co-operation in the harmonisation of radio communications and fingerprint recognition and to assess the problem of cross-border vehicle crime, as well as in higher profile matters such as the generation of good practice in the gathering of terrorist information and the development of the new Europol framework, is testimony to this versatility (Baker, 1992). So, too, is the fact that over the course of its presidency the UK arranged as many as sixty meetings of law enforcement and security officials across a wide range of subject matters, in the process generating so much paperwork as to threaten to overload the Trevi secure fax network[15].

The reasons for this pragmatic and ecumenical approach to co-operation are many and varied. It may in part be connected to the tradition of empire, the legacy of a period when influence was exerted, and discipline frequently imposed, through the design and oversight of colonial policing systems (Brogden, 1987). More positively, it may be connected with the attractiveness of the UK system and the practices it encourages as a model of policing distinct from the dominant continental or 'Roman' model with its philosophy of close central governmental control (Terrill, 1989; Mawby, 1990, ch.2). Relatedly, the relative autonomy from governmental control of the UK police as a professional body (Walker, 1992b) has undoubtedly encouraged the development of a dense network of co-operative contacts and initiatives outwith the rarefied and easily congested channels of formal inter-governmental relations. Whatever the roots of this more productive strain of activity, however, its import may be to make co-operation within the formal EC framework less rather than more attractive. Thus, quite apart from its more immediate political context and implications, another reason why the Communitarian path may be followed somewhat reluctantly by UK politicians and professionals is that its timetable is too slow and uncertain and its territorial remit too inflexible to meet perceived demand and to take advantage of perceived opportunities (Birch, 1992).

Accordingly, a complex mix of general political factors and arguments specific to policing and criminal justice policy suggest that, despite its initial endorsement at the Maastricht negotiations, the UK Government is at best ambivalent in its attitudes towards Europol as a vehicle for a more comprehensive framework of co-operation in the longer term. Perhaps, as has been indicated on certain occasions, the idea mooted earlier of a wider Europol relatively free from the central decision making structures of the EC may be viewed more favourably (Boys Smith, 1991) or, as has attracted significant support in the policy-making circles of ACPO, a more central role for Interpol will be sought (Birch, 1992). However, an overriding concern to maintain flexibility of response may militate against too pronounced an emphasis upon any particular co-operative structure, even those structures which, as in the two cases just cited, may be designed to provide a fairly permissive framework for their members rather than impose authoritative direction upon them.

Evaluation

Having looked at the background to UK involvement in international police co-operation and the direction of current trends, how do we evaluate present arrangements? In order to assess this in a systematic manner, we must separate out the various different dimensions of the question. One distinction concerns the evaluative criterion to be applied - effectiveness or accountability? The other concerns the territorial dimension of the question to be addressed - international or national - since the impact of international policing arrangements depends not only upon the international designs themselves, but also upon how those arrangements fit with the domestic policing system. If we run these two sets of considerations together, we produce a matrix of four issues to be addressed: the effectiveness of international arrangements, the accountability of international arrangements, the effectiveness of national arrangements, and the accountability of national arrangements. As we shall see, although their initial separation is analytically useful, these matters remain complexly interrelated in practice.

The International Dimension: Effectiveness

If we begin by looking at the effectiveness of arrangements at the international level, of all aspects of our evaluation of the UK's involvement in international policing, this is the most difficult to frame in terms of a concrete set of tests or standards. There are a number of reasons for this. In the first place, as we have seen, the precise nature and dimensions of the problem of international crime and insecurity are controversial and so the standards against which to judge the effectiveness of police co-operation remain elusive. Secondly, as the major proposals which will guide international police co-operation in the next few years are either still on the drawing board or only at an early stage of implementation, there is very little by way of evidence to inform our assessment of their relative merits. In the third place, it is in any case arguable that, unless and until international co operation reaches a stage where the dominant police function in a community is exercised at the supranational rather than the national level[16], effectiveness in the international arena will depend more upon national factors and so will remain more susceptible to a 'bottom up' analysis.

The fact that criteria and models of good practice in the international domain remain contested and undeveloped means that it would be premature to attempt a definitive evaluation of present arrangements and a detailed set of proposals for future development. We can nevertheless gain a more indirect purchase on the question of effectiveness from two angles. First, precisely because the present debate is so fluid and controversial it is vital to ensure that the methods by which it is pursued and developed are well informed and that there is adequate representation not merely of those groups with a predominantly security-orientated perspective, but also of all other interested constituencies. We will return to this issue in the conclusion to this chapter. Secondly, and more concretely, notwithstanding ongoing controversy over the ultimate ends of international policing, we can identify certain key organisational choices which recur in discussion and development of co-operative arrangements. These, too, have a definite, if more subtle, bearing upon issues of effectiveness and may be scrutinised in these terms without prejudice to the question of ultimate ends.

These organisational choices tend to revolve around a cluster of closely related variables which can be mapped onto a single continuum. At one pole there is a conception of international police organisation as a *highly integrated* set of arrangements. The emphasis here is upon an institutional framework with general jurisdiction across the range of international crime problems, which merges policy, operational and operational support (training, officer exchange schemes etc.) functions, and which declares a clear hierarchy of significance between different territorial levels of organisation. At the other pole there is a conception of international policing as a *loosely structured* set of arrangements. By contrast, the emphasis here is upon the maintenance of organisational boundaries between different functional specialisms and different strategic levels, and upon the co-existence of régimes of equivalent status pitched at different territorial levels. Our earlier overview suggests that in terms of these criteria, international police co-operation in the European arena sits somewhere between these two extremes. The advent of Europol and Schengen and to some extent even the development of Interpol indicate growing support for a more integrated solution, but the very fact of their rival claims tends to undermine this objective (Van Reenen; 1989, (Bigo, 1992). In any case, as we have seen, there are many interested parties, including UK governmental and professional interests, whose support for such institutions is conditional on their not being accorded monopoly status. Given this intermediate position, therefore, what are the relative advantages or disadvantages of movement in either direction along the continuum?

In terms of effectiveness it is arguable that a more integrated approach would avoid wasteful overlap and competition, facilitate pooling of information and co-ordination of effort within and between law enforcement sectors, allow a productive interaction between policy and operations and provide a dominant institutional framework as a focal point for public and professional legitimation. A loosely structured approach, on the other hand, while less advantageous on these counts, may be preferable on other grounds. It may allow the retention and development of specialist expertise; facilitate a more comprehensive and flexible response in the various different territorial contexts within which international crime patterns unfold; and through permitting policy and operations each their separate institutional domain, avoid the opposite dangers of strategic policy considerations being consistently displaced by immediate operational imperatives. Alternatively it may avoid operational decisions being entirely dictated by the broader political climate. Finally, it may prevent the development of a complacent bureaucratic monolith geared to protect its own vested interests.

Merely to articulate these alternative possibilities is to underline how speculative any investment in new organisational forms is bound to be. It is a question of fine judgement and balance whether any particular package will be conducive to the pursuit of effective policies against international crime. Indeed, it may be that what is optimally required at any particular stage of development would, in the broadest structural terms, resemble what we presently have (albeit, largely by default rather than design), namely a mixed system, with elements of both a highly integrated and a loosely structured approach. One instance of the philosophy underpinning the mixed system approach as it currently operates is the attitude of the present UK Government towards Europol. This appears to combine support for a general jurisdiction in a functional sense (anti-terrorism remaining a key exception), with continuing advocacy of a variety of overlapping territorial régimes. Of course, if a hybrid approach was considered in a more systematic transnational manner, it might yield a more general model of optimal organisational structure. It is arguable, for example, that functional specialism may preserve expertise and also respect the semi-autonomous domains of policy and operations, without simultaneously sacrificing co-ordination, provided that a sectoral approach is confined to operational matters and that these operational units are in turn under the general control of a policy making unit which is itself more tightly integrated.

Developing these propositions into a more concrete design, one could envisage a model of Europol as the dominant international police organisation in its region, with a unified policy-making core surrounded by various tentacles performing limited operational functions in matters such as information exchange, crime pattern analysis, co-ordination of national investigations, training, technological developments etc, with some further sub-division in terms of crime-subject area. In the final analysis, therefore, issues of organisational choice undoubtedly do have a bearing upon questions of effectiveness, but we must be prepared to go beyond crude dichotomies and investigate and experiment with the finer details of organisational design in order to develop this line of inquiry.

The International Dimension: Accountability

The difficulties of organisational choice at the most general level are equally apparent if we turn to our second standard of evaluation, namely accountability. Again, both the highly integrated and the loosely structured approaches display some characteristics which are conducive to the establishment of adequate standards of accountability and others which are less so. The highly integrated approach has the advantage of providing a clear focus upon a single institutional structure from which all lines of accountability should flow. Equally, to confer monopoly or dominant police power in the international field on a single institution carries corresponding disadvantages. Its scale of operations, range of legal capacities, complexity of internal structure and inevitable development of vested professional interests may render it less susceptible to external control, even if the organisation is restricted to certain focal concerns. Further, if we remind ourselves of the seductive professional and political attractions of the creation of an open ended 'internal security field' in this domain (Bigo, 1992), it may be difficult to confine within its formal remit an integrated organisation which boasts significant resources and to curb its efforts to colonise related policy and operational domains.

The loosely structured approach, on the other hand, has the advantage of establishing an internal and ever-shifting balance of power which prevents any single institution from consolidating a dominant power base and developing mechanisms to insulate itself from external control. Equally, it has the countervailing disadvantage of presenting a more fragmented, less settled and less transparent institutional field upon which accountability mechanisms require to be targeted. If we balance these considerations, perhaps a hybrid model along the lines indicated above again emerges as the most attractive option, in that a single, albeit loosely structured organisation provides a relatively clear focus for accountability while being less likely than a centralised organisation to shield itself from external influences and develop entrenched attitudes and interests in the conduct of its operations.

However, while the relationship between organisational form and degree of accountability is complex and any suggestions for optimal organisational design in this regard are necessarily tentative, this need not exhaust our evaluation of existing institutions in terms of accountability standards. Unlike effectiveness, the idea of accountability speaks to general principles which are not context-dependent and which may be measured by identifiable and reliable means supplied by the analyst. Accordingly, we are not handicapped, as in the case of the standard of effectiveness, by the relative underdevelopment of practice in the international domain. We can, therefore, move beyond the broad dilemmas of organisational choice and argue that the adequacy of accountability arrangements is best tested by the presence or absence of certain concrete mechanisms of external influence, irrespective of how loosely structured or highly integrated is the institutional environment in which they are located.

Drawing upon Baldwin's analysis (Baldwin, 1987), we may argue that there are three formal means whereby the accountability, in its broadest sense, of an institutional activity such as policing may be assessed. The first concerns the extent to which the institution and its practices are authorised by a legislative mandate. The second concerns the arrangements made for holding the institution to regular account by a broad democratic constituency. The third concerns matters of 'due process', rules and procedures whereby individuals and groups affected by specific institutional practices may influence such practices or otherwise ensure that their interests are safeguarded in the pursuit of these practices.

Legislative Mandate

Whereas most national policing systems, including the UK's, have statutory underpinnings, albeit typically significantly open textured, this has been largely lacking in the European and broader international domain. Interpol, although now recognised as having the status of an inter-governmental organisation, is notorious for its lack of a Treaty basis in international law (Anderson, 1989); Trevi has operated outwith the EC Treaty framework, while for all its detail, the regulatory régime associated with Schengen is one of international law rather than directly applicable EC law. Finally, even Europol, although recognised within the EC Treaty framework under the Maastricht agreement, will operate at the margins of the main EC institutions. In particular, the more detailed legislative mandate which is in the process of being formulated to govern its future development and operations, will be a creature of international law with the European Commission holding no power of initiative (Art. K.3.).

Popular Accountability Controls

Stemming from this weak legislative base, popular accountability controls over the relevant institutions are equally supine. Neither Interpol nor Trevi has to account to a separate agency across the broad range of its functions. A Joint Supervisory Authority will monitor Schengen, but only in respect of activities associated with the Technical Support Function and the SIS; further, since the Supervisory Authority comprises representatives from the national authorities involved in implementing the agreement, it lacks both supranational status and independence from the system it is required to oversee. As regards Europol also, it has been decided that the main lines of accountability will follow an attenuated course through existing national structures (Trevi, 1991). This may to some extent be compensated for by the role of the European Parliament, which under the new Treaty of Maastricht has the right to be informed and consulted about developments by the Presidency and the Commission and to ask questions of, and make recommendations to, the Council (Art. K.6).

On its recent record, the European Parliament can be expected to exercise this function with some vigilance. Its growing awareness of the increasing criminal justice dimension of Community activity led it to institute in January 1992 a new Committee for Civil Liberties and Internal Affairs, which has already produced a number of useful reports in this area (Van Outrive, 1992a, 1992b, 1992c, 1992d; Tsimas, 1992), in turn stimulating lively debates and the passage of critical resolutions in the full Parliament. Additionally, a separate Committee of Inquiry reported to Parliament on the question of the spread of drugs related organised crime in April 1992. Despite these successes, the enthusiasm of the European Parliament is in danger of outstripping its legal powers, as was graphically illustrated by the recent failure of a Green MEP to obtain substantive answers to any of the 65 detailed written questions he had submitted to the Council of Ministers on the workings of Trevi (Jenkins, 1992). The reason given for refusal was the absence of competence on the part of the Council in these matters and, since even in a post Maastricht regime the powers of the Council and Commission will remain limited. The Parliament may be similarly obstructed in its future attempts to gain enlightenment from the Community's executive leadership (Miller, 1992).

Due process

If we turn to the final method of accountability, namely due process
protections, again the various safeguards are underdeveloped.
International police co operation as it is presently practiced is
already capable of impinging significantly upon individual rights
and freedoms, especially in the field of computerised information
exchange. At the present stage of co- operation, where forms of
operational aid short of joint organisational capacity are being
developed to deal with a perceived increase in the international
security deficit, information technology systems have assumed a
pivotal pioneering function as methods of practical co operation
which are not necessarily restricted to specialist police groups.

The range of proposed or recently established international
information systems is thus almost as broad as that of new police
agencies. Interpol underwent an extensive computerisation
programme in the 1980s and, following its move to new 'high tech'
headquarters in Lyons in 1989, it has recently established an
automated search facility allowing direct access by member states
to a central pool of criminal intelligence, subject only to restrictions
imposed by the supplier country (Harrison, 1992; Kendall, 1992).
The Schengen Information System (SIS), which is to be based at
Strasbourg, will include information not only on wanted and
convicted persons but also on undesirable aliens and persons whom
it is suspected may commit serious crime in the future (Den Boer,
1991). Other major information technology initiatives include
Trevi's proposed European Information System, which is similar in
conception to the SIS and the Customs Information System, which,
when it becomes fully operational in October 1993, will provide a
database and network for the pooling and exchange of information
amongst European Customs Officers on drugs smuggling, fraudulent
export certificates, illegal trafficking in arms, endangered species,
etc (Miles, 1993).

As Jenkins has documented, even before most of these ambitious
designs have been implemented there is a worrying incidence of
reported cases of individuals who have been subject to oppressive

police treatment or are at risk of interference from law enforcement authorities as a result of false information being relayed about them across national borders and not subsequently being corrected (Jenkins, 1992). When systematic computer links between national forces are set up there must be a concern that the incidence of such abuses will increase exponentially. Under such a régime will assume a spurious objectivity in the eyes of those to whom it is disseminated. Finally, those who receive information relayed transnationally may well lack awareness of the wider context within which the computerised text was produced and which is necessary for its adequate interpretation (Jenkins, 1992).

Against this background, existing safeguards seem insufficiently robust. Interpol has a rudimentary complaints system in the form of a Supervisory Board to examine internal files, although substantial internal control is retained over its membership (Anderson, 1989, 65-66). More generally, all EC Member States are signatories to the 1981 European Convention on Data Protection and the 1987 Recommendation on the use of personal data in the police sector, both of which contain provisions pertinent to the various computerised information systems mentioned above. However, both instruments allow wide scope for derogation in matters of state security, public safety and crime prevention, and so their capacity to prevent abuses in individual cases is correspondingly reduced (Baldwin-Edwards and Hebenton, 1992; Norman, 1992; Raab, 1992). Moreover, in an area dominated by developments within the EC, what is conspicuous by its absence is a specifically EC dimension in response. A draft Directive on Data Protection was published in 1990 but it is unclear whether and when it will receive final legislative endorsement and whether and to what extent police files will fall under its protective canopy in any event (Raab, 1992). Instead, the continuing lacunae has recently prompted the Committee on Civil Liberties and Internal Affairs of the European Parliament to call for the appointment by the Commission of a Community Data Protection Officer (Van Outrive, 1992c, 8).

Concern about the protection of civil liberties, of course, is not confined to the issue of data protection. If Europol were to acquire

operational powers, including those of search, questioning and
arrest, the need for rights of due process would become even more
pressing. In such circumstances, it is arguable that, as with many
domestic systems (Goldsmith, 1991), what would be required as
well as a detailed set of procedural rights[17], would be a special
complaints process and tribunal through which such rights could be
effectively vindicated. Here again, the European Parliament has been
prominent in advocating reform, resolving in response to a report
received from its Committee on Civil Liberties and Internal Affairs
(Van Outrive, 1992d) that Europol should be treated as a
Community body against which individual complaints might be
made to the new European Ombudsman provided for in the Treaty
of Maastricht[18].

Scope for Reform

Why are current accountability standards so deficient and what
prospects are there for improvement? To answer these questions it
is necessary to return to the theoretical source from which our
analysis of the three forms of accountability is derived. In Baldwin's
original argument each of the three forms corresponded to a
particular type of claim to legitimacy which could be made on
behalf of an institution. Alongside these formal legal or
constitutional sources, he identified two other practical bases of
legitimacy, namely expertise and institutional efficiency and
effectiveness.

Arguably, if we shift our focus to these practical criteria, we
encounter the developing institutions of international policing on
much stronger ground. Like many public service organisations,
domestic police institutions seek to enhance their occupational status
and justify their decision making autonomy by reference to a
specialist 'knowledge mandate' (Halliday, 1985). If policing is
perceived as a matter of technical skill, then its practitioners are
more likely to be treated as respected 'professionals' and less likely
to be subjected to close scrutiny (Holdaway, 1983; Brogden,
Jefferson and Walklate, 1988, 80-84). Of course, this claim is made
with greater and lesser degrees of persuasiveness (Baldwin, 1987,

101). It is, however, in those very areas associated with developments in international crime and policing, that it is most likely to be effective. Crimes of terrorism, drug trafficking, money laundering, art fraud etc, have traditionally been tackled by specialist units each of which claims to possess its own particular brand of esoteric knowledge and to have its own particular, and necessarily confidential, sources and techniques of criminal intelligence. Such claims, irrespective of whether they are in principle defensible, are by their nature difficult to rebut and so tend to assume a self-justifying quality.

Relatedly, European policing institutions may also be well placed to attract public support, or at least to minimise criticism, on grounds of efficiency and effectiveness. As we have seen in earlier chapters, in the post-war years police institutions in many Western democracies have become increasingly unable to defend their performance in terms of their traditional, symbolically potent core role of crime prevention and detection (Manning, 1977; Punch, 1985; Reiner, 1992; Platt, 1987; Guyomarch, 1991). Instead, the seemingly inexorable rise of recorded crime rates has rendered domestic police forces increasingly vulnerable to value for money scrutiny. One response to this favoured by some professionals and politicians has been to attempt to redefine the role of the police in more modest terms, as one party to a much wider social contract to set and maintain acceptable levels of public tranquillity (Reiner, 1991a). However, the corollary of reduced standard of public expectations may be a 'much lower pedestal' (Reiner, 1991a) for the police in terms of social standing and their capacity to win scarce public resources.

Accordingly, the image of the police as the primary custodians of law and order remains potentially attractive and continues to be emphasised in particular areas of crime which are deemed such significant threats to social order that a narrow audit of cost effectiveness arguably provides an impoverished measure of the value of the police contribution. Again, as argued earlier, a number of key areas within the international policing domain, in particular terrorism and drugs fall into this category. When these matters are interwoven into a single ideological fabric, a homogeneous 'internal security field', the apocalyptic metaphor of the police as a 'thin blue line' holding firm against chaos develops a powerful resonance and threatens to marginalise more mundane considerations of efficiency (McLaughlin, 1992; Dorn, Murji and South, 1992).

Now, arguably, the relatively favourable prospects of nascent international policing institutions in terms of practical legitimacy in comparison to their poor standing in terms of formal legitimacy (and the accountability mechanisms through which this is typically supplied) is no mere accident of circumstance. Rather, there is a causal link between the two and this link both helps to account for the poverty of present accountability mechanisms and indicates why the establishment of institutions of accountability at the international level may continue to meet with apathy or resistance. The nub of this argument is that the supportive relationship between formal legitimacy and practical legitimacy is generally more tenuous in the domain of international policing than it would typically be within the domestic domain. The reasons for this are twofold.

First, the very nature of the practical arguments which presently ground police legitimacy in the international domain are such that it is difficult to test them against objective standards. Arguments about technical expertise and against the utility of quantifiable indices of efficiency and effectiveness achieve a form of ideological closure. They are socially effective because they successfully elide questions about the validity of their premises, not because they answer them.

Secondly, whereas in many domestic policing systems, there is a symbiosis between the practical and formal grounds of legitimacy which necessitates some care being taken with the health of both, this is not the case in the international domain. Put simply, domestic police forces typically require a steady flow of information from all sections of the public in order to exploit their expertise and achieve acceptable standards of effectiveness in crime fighting. This information flow, however, is dependent upon a high level of mutual trust between police and public which, in turn, is at least partly dependent upon public confidence that the police are properly answerable through constitutional mechanisms (Kinsey, Lea and Young, 1986 ch.2).

In the international system, on the other hand, this vital nexus between effectiveness, active consent and public answerability is much less well established. Particular sections of the public may be crucial informants within networks associated with supranational policing but the public as a whole is not such a vital resource. Further, the practical arguments for according legitimacy to supranational institutions tend to emphasise their need for decision making autonomy so as not to compromise their efficiency and dilute their expertise. Insofar as such arguments are endorsed by the general public, the scope for strong constitutional controls will be seen as limited. Finally, as we are dealing with deviant groups which are particularly marginal to the experiences and sympathies of the majority of he general public, popular sentiment is less likely to be vigilant on behalf of those typically implicated in adversarial encounters with the police in the key areas of supranational policing than it might otherwise be.

In conclusion, therefore, the social and political pressures for police accountability are currently less strong in the international domain than in the national domain. The different relationship which pertains in the international domain between prevalent conceptions of police effectiveness, public perceptions of legitimacy, and the participation of the public in the policing enterprise, entails that there is at present neither a strong sense on the part of professionals and policy-makers of the prudential value of accountability measures, nor a broad groundswell of popular opinion organised to make effective demands in this area. It should be stressed, however, that this does not detract from the intrinsic importance of accountability guarantees in the international domain. These speak to values associated not only with democratic participation but also with the protection of individual and minority rights, values which remain significant regardless of the extent of effectiveness of and public acquiescence in particular policing enterprises. Indeed, in the case of minority rights, the extent to which they are protected against intrusive police activity may vary indirectly with the weight of majoritarian sentiment in favour of the relevant police institutions and practices. If anything, therefore, the relative lack of concerted public pressure for increased accountability currently merely underlines the need for the issues involved to be monitored vigilantly.

The National Dimension: effectiveness

Whereas at the international level, questions of effectiveness tend to be secondary to questions of accountability, if anything the opposite is the case at the national level. While the issue of the ultimate objectives of international policing is no less elusive when viewed from a domestic purpose, there is at least a well developed and well documented set of institutions, practices and attitudes at the domestic level which can be examined for their likely 'fit' with the demands of international policing. On the other hand, the question of accountability, although not unimportant, is perhaps a secondary consideration. As we are concerned with systems of international policing, then the primary mechanisms of accountability are most appropriately located at the international level. Certainly, domestic accountability structures can play an important ancillary role but, particularly where, as in the EC, the political institutions at the international level are in place and capable of development to meet the challenge directly, these local institutions can only ever have an indirect and secondary relevance. To consider otherwise is to endorse a myopic and anachronistic conception of national sovereignty which legitimises the persistence of the 'democratic deficit' at the supranational level and which, indeed, is one of the very arguments which has been invoked to justify the absence of accountability of institutions such as Trevi over the years (Bogdnor, 1991, Bunyan, 1991).

If, then, we turn first to considerations of effectiveness there are certain structural and cultural features of the domestic system which are relevant to this issue. The key structural feature for our purposes is *localism*. It has, of course, been amply documented in previous chapters how this basic organising principle of UK policing has been compromised by a glut of centralising initiatives in recent years (Reiner, 1991b 24-36; Walker, 1991 18-21). Nevertheless, despite many qualifications, the basic organisational unit in the UK police for normal territorial policing is still the local force. In this respect it remains unique in the EC, since all other Member States have a substantial number of police personnel employed within national forces, albeit often within a decentralised format (Home Affairs Committee, 1990, xvi-xvii).

This resilient core of localism poses a number of problems for the effectiveness of international police co-operation. To begin with, it has tended to militate against an integrated approach to policy-making in the new international arena with individual forces, specialist units, officers' associations, local authority associations and the Home Office often speaking with different voices. The efforts of the International Affairs Advisory Committee (IAAC) of the Association of Chief Police Offices (ACPO) in the three years since its inception have gone some way to filling this lacuna at the professional level at least, although in the final analysis the committee lacks executive authority and so must operate through negotiation and informal persuasion.

Although the committee was instrumental, in the instigation of the practice whereby the 'British Police Service' submits evidence to official inquiries as a single unit and approaches policy matters with a common front (Gregory, 1991,46), to sustain this united approach on an informal footing in the longer term depends upon the unlikely eventuality that there can be secured a reasonable harmony of views between different levels and parts of the service on each and every major policy issue. Thus, the terms of reference of the Sheehy Inquiry into Police Responsibilities and Rewards, which was appointed in July 1992, address so intimately the differences in status, renumeration and job content of different ranks that the various officer organisations have to some extent reverted to the practice of identifying with their own sectional interests in the ensuing public debate, and in particular have prepared separate evidence for the Inquiry[19]; likewise, if a similarly divisive theme were to emerge in the international arena, here too there would be no institutional safeguards to prevent the subsequent fracturing of professional opinion.

If we turn to the subject of operational co-ordination, it is noteworthy that the new ACPO Committee has proven flexible enough to perform a role in this context also; for example, where previously there was no uniform procedure, all requests for the secondment of UK police officers abroad are now channelled through this committee[20]. Two organisational initiatives of greater significance in the area of operational co-ordination are the UK Central Authority for Mutual Legal Assistance in Criminal Matters and the National Criminal Intelligence Service (NCIS). The first mentioned body was established within the Home Office in June 1991 as a central clearing house for requests to and from the UK under Part 1 of the Criminal Justice (International Co-operation) Act 1990 (which gives effect to the UK's Treaty obligations under the Council of Europe Convention on Mutual Legal Assistance). As intimated earlier, the second body was established in April 1992 to co-ordinate various national intelligence functions, many of which have a strong international flavour such as the Interpol NCB and the network of domestic and foreign liaison officers within its Drugs Division (previously NDIU).

Despite their strategic significance, however, the powers of these bodies are limited: they provide what is essentially a service function for local forces and so tend to be in a position to encourage rather than to demand standard practice. Different forces, for example, have always demonstrated different attitudes and approaches to the utility of the UK NCB as a conduit for the passage of international criminal information, (Home Affairs Committee, 1990, xxviii-xxix) and whether the location of the NCB within a more versatile and operationally less marginal national organisation will help it to attain a better general reputation and promote greater uniformity of practice is a moot point. At a more fundamental level, the vulnerable standing of an agency such as NCIS as an optional facility, rather than an authoritative centre within an organisational structure marked by localism, is underlined by the fact that even the most basic question of whether the Scottish forces and the RUC should become full participants in its new institutional network has been the subject of protracted negotiations[21].

The one major dimension of international crime which does not fall under the aegis of NCIS, namely terrorism, arguably provides a yet more striking example of the failure of co-ordination, a failure which in this case straddles policy and operational levels. Recent discussion has centred upon the replacement of the Metropolitan Police Special Branch by the Security Service (MI5) as the lead agency in gathering intelligence on the IRA in mainland Britain, a change which was announced in May 1992[22]. However, this should not obscure the fact that there are still a plethora of different agencies, mostly locally based, involved in the overall anti-terrorist thrust. These include, apart from the two mentioned, the Metropolitan anti-terrorist unit, the Special Branch of all territorial forces outside London, and the Regional Crime Squads. It is in contemplation of this unwieldy set of arrangements that the Chief Constable of the RUC, Sir Hugh Annesley, has recently called for the establishment of a national anti-terrorist unit[23].

As a further consequence of localism, the establishment of a fair system of representation of regional interests within key international agencies has also been controversial. For instance, the RUC has complained about its lack of representation on Trevi 1, the Trevi Working Group specifically concerned with terrorism, despite its significant operational involvement in this area (Home Affairs Committee, 1990, xxxviii). Greater police involvement in the Trevi working group framework, which has been another achievement of ACPO IAAC, has improved matters recently but the sheer range of regional and functional interests is such that arguments as to the adequacy of representation are likely to continue. There have, for example, been complaints that the Trevi 'troika', a support staff supplied by the immediate past, current and next EC Presidency which has an important agenda setting role, does not adequately consult the spectrum of police views articulated in the Working Groups[24]. Indeed, this continuing dissatisfaction with political institutions may also partly explain the recent efforts of ACPO

IAAC in attempting to establish a Police Council for Europe (or as it has been labelled in a later version, a Police Programme for Europe,) as an exclusively professional discussion forum (Bentham, 1991; Evans, 1992).

Finally, as the somewhat moderate success of the force International Liaison Officer network has demonstrated, the decentralised framework of UK policing also creates difficulties in respect of the assimilation and dissemination of information and knowledge about the policing implications of the 1992 programme and other broad developments relevant to international criminal justice. When first established in 1990, the liaison officer scheme was a joint ACPO/Metropolitan Police initiative and thus its uneven impact could to some extent be attributed to its ambiguous lines of authority (Gorry, 1991). However, even now that the ACPO secretariat has assumed full responsibility there remain inconsistencies and blockages and an uneven utilisation of the official communications channel[25], problems which are attributable to the attenuated lines of communication and the absence of a clear hierarchy implicit in a locally organised system.

Moving on to questions of occupational attitudes, we can identify an additional set of impediments to co-operation in various cultural tensions which affect the police service and other law enforcement agencies. The secrecy and solidarity of small units and working groups which has been noted in numerous studies of policework (Skolnick, 1975, ch.3; Reiner, 1992, ch.3) assumes a broad significance in the context of international policing. First, as the front line activities associated with international policing are dispersed across an unusually wide range of narrow specialist tasks organised into different departments, or even, as in the case of the specialist border services (HM Customs and HM Immigration Service), allocated to distinct organisational entities, the different traditions, working practices and information networks of these different specialisms may lead to rivalry and disharmony. Secondly, as the gulf in organisational status, experience and understanding between policy-making and monitoring on the one hand and operational implementation on the other may be more pronounced in the international arena than in the area of purely domestic policing, the propensity of 'street cops' to resist or modify the designs of 'management cops' is increased accordingly (Reuss-Ianni and Ianni, 1983). Thirdly, as the solidarity of police officers is, *inter alia*, a territorial solidarity (Holdaway, 1983, ch.4) and one which depends upon a sense of doing the same work and sharing the same problems (Skolnick, 1975, 52), the extent to which operational units based in different countries and operating in social environments largely unknown to one another can work together on a basis of mutual trust and respect is uncertain.

That these are not merely speculative hypotheses is apparent from criticism typically levelled against Interpol, as unduly slow and cumbersome and as a less than comprehensive source and repository of information (Home Affairs Committee, 1990, xxv xxvii). Such charges are in part due to a domestic preference for informal channels of communication, which reflects an impatience with and wariness of procedures which demand a set course of action and a detailed documentation record that may subsequently be exposed to the critical scrutiny of senior officers. They are also partly attributable to an unwillingness to expedite inquiries by responding promptly to impersonal requests for assistance from abroad, reflecting the low priority given to the needs of those outwith an officer's operational frame of reference.

How might the structural and cultural impediments to effectiveness which we have identified be overcome? In the case of the idea of localism, the search for increased effectiveness at the international level might dictate a much more explicit offensive against the principle in key sectoral domains. The problem here, however, is that there is no obvious and neat divide between issues whose major dimension is national and those whose major dimension is local. Anti-terrorism may be one clear example of a law enforcement practice where each operation can only be understood in a national and international context. It is a 'high policing' issue (Brodeur, 1983, p.513), one which poses a systematic threat to the dominant social and political order within states and which must be responded to in those terms. However, the same could not be said of various other crimes with a significant national and international profile (Walker, 1992a, Den Boer and Walker, 1993). To take the example of drugs related offences, localism may still be a valuable standard to apply in this sector inasmuch as it permits neighbourhood discretion to experiment with different types of preventive campaigns and enforcement strategies. And if this threatens to compromise the role of a national agency such as NCIS in the co-ordination of overall operational strategy, then hard choices, or at least careful accommodations, may be required between competing structural principles.

Returning to the cultural problems identified earlier, again structural reform promises a measure of improvement. For example, the difficulties associated with the traditional functional division of labour between services and specialisms in the frontline of international police co-operation may be tackled by providing new umbrella organisations within which co-operative relations can be cultivated, as with NCIS which employs police officers alongside customs officers in its Drugs Division, and also the Serious Fraud Office, within which seconded police officers work with accountants and lawyers. In many other cases, however, the relationship between cultural pattern and structural arrangement is less obvious, and attempts at reform will have to proceed in a tentative manner. This is particularly so given limited domestic experience of the ways in which practical problems might manifest themselves, the geographical position of the UK having minimised previous operational exposure to intensive and recurrent co- operation, and in particular having precluded any experience of close border co-operation between national forces.

Accordingly, the policing of the channel tunnel, the one case where a system of 'hands on' co-operation is inevitable and imminent, offers a crucial experiment in addressing the detailed cultural issues involved in future co operation. Unsurprisingly, it is already throwing up organisational dilemmas which reflect the tensions indicated above. It appears from interviews with the officers involved[26] that the debate within Kent police over the proper role of its European Liaison Unit, which is but one component in a wider programme of organisational reform undertaken by the force in anticipation of its new border role (Harding, 1991; Gallagher, 1992), divides between those who see it as a main conduit for operational exchanges, and those for whom it is no more than a supplement to a much denser flow of exchanges between operational officers from both ends. The choices which present themselves here - formal versus informal networking, vertically organised versus horizontally organised lines of responsibility, co-ordination and communication etc., - are directly informed by understandings of the peculiarities of occupational culture enumerated above. Indeed very similar choices are likely to recur, and similar attention to underlying cultural difficulties and dilemmas be demanded if, and when, the attempt is made in years to come to operationalise more ambitious co-operative initiatives.

National Level: Accountability

If we turn to the question of accountability at the national level for international policing arrangements, the problems which arise essentially track those identified as relevant to questions of effectiveness. First, then, we may consider how the principle of localism affects accountability considerations. It has been argued from a number of sources that the acceleration of the *de facto* centralising tendency in British policing, a significant contributory factor to which has been the range of domestic initiatives in international police co-operation, has underlined the problem of the absence of adequate means to bring the new central entities to democratic account (Spencer, 1990, ch.7; Bunyan, 1991; McLaughlin, 1992). Thus, just as the formally decentralised structure of the UK police creates problems of effective direction of effort *within* the law enforcement community, it also generates difficulties for bodies attempting to exert *external* influence. From a defensively oriented professional perspective, therefore, it may seem ironical that the very factors which militate against internal cohesion serve also to shield internal discretion from external monitoring. While this irony might leave some insiders ambivalent about the establishment of *de jure* national structures if this implies their possessing their own dedicated accountability mechanisms,

(Jenkins, 1992; McLaughlin, 1991) from our perspective this gap instead merely reinforces the arguments for structural reform. Indeed, the establishment alongside NCIS of a Steering Group containing a certain level of democratic representation provides a modest vindication of the value of formal institutional recognition of centralising trends.

Further, if we anticipate a broader process of organisational transformation acknowledging the need to balance local with national structures in accordance with the arguments as to effectiveness outlined earlier, more general accountability mechanisms at the national level - whether through the Home Secretary and Parliament, or a new National Police authority comprising local representatives, or both - would be required. Alongside any role they might have in respect of purely domestic policing, they would also provide a distinctive UK input to complement whatever supranational devices were developed within the overall system for supervising international policing.

Finally, if we return to the cultural impediments mentioned earlier, we must recognise that, even if we develop policies and evolve structures on the basis of improved understanding and anticipation of operational responses, it may still prove impossible to overcome cultural obstacles to the achievement of certain objectives. In these circumstances the difficulty would not be one of lack of knowledge or imagination on the part of policy- makers but the more intractable matter of competing normative priorities, coupled with the impracticality of imposing a particular solution in a 'top-down' fashion. Just as behaviour and attitudes within a rank and file culture characterised by low visibility and significant street level discretion (Wilson, 1968, 7) have often proved ultimately resistant to reform attempts, so too they may in some cases prove impervious to measures in the domain of international practice. In the final analysis, therefore, unless they are matched by internal consultation and accountability measures which successfully command and 'co-opt' the loyalty and commitment of junior ranks (Reiner, 1992, 221), external accountability controls may be rendered academic by operational subversion of the mandate which they are designed to monitor.

Conclusion

The present chapter has been long on description and diagnosis and somewhat shorter on prescription. This, however, should not be read as an indication that international police institutions and practices are incapable of significant improvement, either because they have already attained an optimal standard or because it is impossible to conceive of practical means whereby improvement may be brought about. As should be apparent from the previous pages, either conclusion would be well wide of the mark.

On the one hand, present international policing arrangements can indeed be subjected to critical analysis, both in terms of their effectiveness and their accountability. Thus, it has been argued that an *ad hoc* approach to questions of institutional design has hampered the development of an effective model of international police organisation; that the peculiarly attenuated relationship which applies in the international domain between practical achievement, public consent and participation, and institutional control, has impeded the development of robust accountability mechanisms; and that the principle of localism has to some extent undermined the domestic contribution to the effectiveness of international co-operation. It has also been argued that certain cultural divisions within the law enforcement enterprise threaten to exacerbate this and that these same structural and cultural characteristics of the domestic scene also detract from the prospects of locally situated accountability controls.

On the other hand, suggestions have been made to improve the present situation, the central theme of which is the need, within careful limits, to develop a greater degree of centralisation and integration of practice at both the national and the international levels in order that co-operation activities can be more effectively co-ordinated and a clearer focus can be provided for accountability mechanisms. More specifically, it has been advocated that, at the level of overall structural design, an arrangement which endorses Europol as the dominant international police organisation within its region, with a unified policy making core connected to a number of modest operational tentacles, might provide the optimal balance in terms of effectiveness and accountability. Secondly, I have argued that international accountability demands a range of different mechanisms, from broad political controls to 'due process' controls such as the Community Data Protection Officer and Ombudsman recently mooted by the European Parliament. Thirdly, I concluded that the effectiveness of the domestic contribution to international police practice may demand, on the one hand, a more systematic commitment to national arrangements in respect of certain functions in order to overcome the organisational dysfunctions of localism, and on the other, the cultivation of umbrella organisations pooling personnel from different agencies and the development of clear and effective channels of communications within and between organisations, in order to counter problems of cultural heterogeneity within the law enforcement enterprise. Finally, it has been argued that accountability arrangements at the national level need to be developed to shadow the new national structures and to provide a domestic counterpoint to the international framework of accountability.

The accent here is still on general themes but this does not imply that a more precise agenda for the development and reform cannot be contemplated. Rather, at the present stage, with many new arrangements still at the point of conception or in their infancy, and the overall dynamic of change difficult to grasp, such an agenda would be premature. Instead, two other interrelated matters must take priority at this stage. First, in a rapidly changing environment there is a basic problem of knowledge and understanding. What is required is a greater appreciation of the broader picture and the problems and possibilities which it poses for efforts to develop a defensible vision of international policing. Hopefully, the present discussion has shed some light upon these wider concerns. Secondly, and here considerations of effectiveness and accountability are joined, there is also required at the political level the development of mechanisms within both national and supranational domains which ensure that all parties with an interest in so doing can contribute in a systematic manner to the shaping of the agenda for future international police co-operation.

As the analysis presented in this chapter indicates, the twin dangers currently exist that policy continues to emerge as a series of incremental shifts and *ad hoc* adjustments by a disparate group of political and professional bodies operating without any explicit long term conception of the ends of international policing in a twilight world of political accountability; and that this process, by excluding a variety of other key constituencies, will through a mixture of design and default encourage a drift towards an authoritarian perspective which establishes security as the predominant value across a very broad policy spectrum. In the final analysis, therefore, while it is important to ensure that the mechanisms through which the new order of international policing will operate encourage effective performance and permit maximum accountability, whether a satisfactory overall system will in fact develop depends upon more immediate contingencies. Unless open and rational decision making procedures are applied to the present stage of policy generation, then it may be that the 'key practice' of international policing (Cain, 1978,158; McLaughlin, 1992, 485) will be allowed to develop along lines which recognise only the most narrowly circumscribed standards of good practice and indices of effectiveness and which harbour a chronic resistance to public scrutiny.

What, however, are the realistic prospects for the broadening of the forum for discussion at this vital formative stage of policy making? At the domestic level, the Government's decision to conduct a review of accountability and overall structure as a purely internal exercise alongside the two external reviews of the criminal justice system (Runciman Royal Commission) and police responsibilities and rewards (Sheehy Inquiry) (Travis, 1993), is eloquent testimony to the difficulties which are and will continue to be faced by outside agencies attempting to influence the debate about shaping the British police to meet new international demands. At least, however, there are in the national context a number of tried and tested institutional structures of a general nature through which opposition may be voiced and alternative views may be articulated, including Parliament and its committees, the local authorities, and in an age where there is growing professional ambivalence about Governmental policy on policing, even the police officer associations. At the supranational level, however, the democratic deficit as it pertains to home affairs issues is so profound that even this minimal platform for the discussion of alternative views rests on shaky foundations.

In this regard it is instructive to note the views recently expressed by the European Parliament Committee on Civil Liberties and Internal Affairs on the constitutional foundations of Europol. In an opinion subsequently endorsed by the full Parliament[27], it argues that, despite the exclusion of such matters from the legislative competence of the EC in the Treaty of Maastricht (Art.K.9), it would be possible to use the more general powers of Community institutions granted in Article 235 of the EEC Treaty to legislate on any matter conducive to the attainment of the broad objectives of the EC, in order to set up Europol by means of a Community regulation. The advantage of dealing with the matter within the legislative mainstream of the Community would be that, at this key foundational stage, it would be possible to invoke the normal procedures for the participation of the European Parliament, European Commission and national Parliaments in the EC law making process, and that the jurisdiction of the European Court of Justice to supervise the resulting scheme would also be guaranteed (Van Outrive, 1992d,10-13).

While it is one thing to identify alternative methods of policy-making, it is quite another to generate the political momentum required to adopt them. One consequence we can be sure of, however, is that unless persistent efforts are made in this direction, the final arrangements defining the role of Europol and elaborating its supervisory mechanisms will faithfully reflect the concerns and preferences of the narrow policy-making base.

Notes

1. See interview with the Home Secretary, Kenneth Clarke, in *The Guardian*, 2 July 1992. See also *The Guardian* 3 July 1992 and Trevi (1991).

2. Interview with Chief Constable Roger Birch, Sussex Constabulary, 9 July 1992. Se also van Outrive (1992a). In September 1992 a Steering Group was established at Strasbourg to launch the Europol initiative (see further, note 11 below), but despite this its final location remains undecided.

3. *The Scotsman*, 2 December 1992.

4. This new body has been named the K4 Committee, after the relevant provision of the Maastricht Treaty. See *The Guardian*, 2 February 1993.

5. *The Guardian*, 22 July 1992.

6. *The Guardian*, 22 July 1992. This became known as the 'Bangemann wave', in recognition of the role of the then EC internal market commissioner, Martin Bangemann, in negotiating the original compromise with the UK Home Secretary, Kenneth Clarke and in acknowledgement of the token form of passport display which would be required of intra-community travellers at British ports under its terms. See also *The Times*, 1 January 1993.

7. The European Council in Edinburgh referred to the need to complete the ratification process of the Dublin Asylum Convention, to conclude the External Frontiers Convention, and to complete negotiations on a Convention on the European Information System, before the remaining restrictions on the free movement of travellers within the EC could be removed (para.18). Another factor explaining the extension of the deadline was the failure of the Schengen countries to conclude plans for the implementation of their free movement agreement

by the end of 1992, the major cause of delay being the inability to finalise arrangements for the Schengen Information System. When it became clear at the time of the meeting of EC interior ministers in December 1992 that delay was inevitable for the above reasons, Kenneth Clarke signalled the UK's determination to maintain its prior position by refusing to discuss a programme for the removal of border controls in the longer term (*The Independent*, 2 February 1993). Furthermore, he proposed a more restrictive interpretation of the Bangemann Wave (see note 6 above) than had been assumed to be the case hitherto, by suggesting that the compromise procedure would apply only to entry via seaports, and not airports - the most common method of entry (*Statewatch*, Vol.3 No.1, January - February, 1993, 10). Although some of Mr Clarke's European colleagues were reported to be angered by his intransigence, the Commission continued its relatively conciliatory stance towards the UK in the New Year when at his first press conference the incoming internal market commissioner, Vanni d'Archirafi, stressed the need for progress to be made 'without splits or confrontations' (*The Guardian*, 22 January 1993). For the most recent statement of the Commission's view, which reiterates the difference in principle with the UK but remains non-confrontational, see European Commission (1993).

8. *Financial Times*, 19-20 September 1992. For the UK Government's attitude at the time of the Luxembourg European Council in June 1991, which laid the political groundwork for including the Europol initiative within the Maastricht Treaty, see *The Independent*, 29 June 1991.

9. *The Guardian*, 29 October 1992.

10. This was widely reported to have been one of the last minute concessions through which the Government sought, and succeeded, to persuade waverers amongst its own backbenchers to vote in favour of the paving motion on the floor of the House of Commons on Wednesday 4 November, 1992, which

allowed the Bill incorporating the Maastricht Treaty into UK law to proceed in due course to its Committee Stage.

11. The functional similarity between the Europol and Schengen systems and the manner in which this encourages overlap and rivalry in institutional development was highlighted by the recent decision to establish the Europol Steering Group in Strasbourg in the same building as the Schengen Information System. See Jenkins (1992). Although the Schengen system was not ready to be implemented by the end of 1992 as earlier envisaged (see note 7 above), it is still intended that it will become operational during 1993 (European Council, 1992, para.19), which continues to suggest a quicker rate of progress than is likely in the case of Europol.

12. That the symbolic connection between policing and the nation state remains strong is exemplified by the fact that the Justice and Home Affairs Chapter of the Treaty of Maastricht which, as has been argued, represent a high-water mark in the transfer of policing competence to the supranational level, nevertheless contains a saving provision which specifies that the existing responsibilities of Member States with regard to the maintenance of law and order and the safeguarding of internal security shall be unaffected (Art. K.2 (2)).

13. It is noteworthy, however, that there may be a divergence between professional and political viewpoints on such matters, reflecting the greater need of political élites to be sensitive to the demands of a broader range of public constituencies. Thus, while the Government has remained opposed to such an innovation (HC Debs. 18 June 1992, cols. 1022-1024 per Kenneth Clarke MP), the British Police Service has recently expressed support for the introduction of ID cards (Home Affairs Committee, 1992, 96). See further Walker (1992b).

14. *The Guardian*, 2 July 1992.

15. *The Guardian*, 2 February 1993.

16. For a projection of the future development of the EC which suggests that, on balance, states are unlikely to cede their dominant role in policing to the new centre, see Walker (1992a), Den Boer and Walker (1993). It is, for instance, arguable, that even if in the longer terms the EC assumes most of the attributes of statehood, it is likely, in Schmitter's phrase, to be a 'post-Hobbesian state' (Streeck and Schmitter, 1991; Bryant, 1991), that is, one which is not born of and required to survive through military struggle. Accordingly, the ideologies and institutions associated with such a state are less likely to be preoccupied with issues of internal and external security than is the case with traditional Hobbesian states, and so in turn development of a strong policing role is less likely to be axiomatic.

17. Article 5-7 of the European Convention on Human Rights, which is specifically endorsed in the Justice and Home Affairs Title of the Treaty of Maastricht (Art. K.4.2.), could serve as foundation principles underpinning such procedural rights. It should be noted, however, that the Treaty on European Union leaves it open whether or not the Court of Justice will have jurisdiction over justice and home affairs matters (Art.K.3), and so there may be no effective judicial forum within which such procedural rights may be vindicated. See also note 27 below and associated text.

18. Resolution of the European Parliament on the setting up of Europol (A3-0382/92), 22 January 1993, para.17.

19. See *The Guardian*, 3 November 1991 (reporting ACPO's written submissions) and 4 November 1992 (reporting the Police Federation's written submissions). There are significant differences over rank structure, sick pay, training and education, etc.

20. Interview with Chief Constable Roger Birch, Sussex Constabulary, 9 July 1992.

21. *The Scotsman*, 28 August 1992.

22. *The Observer*, 10 May 1992. This was one of the factors which recently prompted the Home Affairs Committee to call for the Security Service to be made more fully accountable, preferably to the Home Affairs Committee itself (Home Affairs Committee, 1993, paras. 16.28). The fact that there has been greater pressure for this aspect of police and security activity to be made accountable since the main responsibility was transferred to a *de jure* national body adds further support to the argument made at pp.46-48 of the text concerning the general relationship between national organisations and accountability.

23. Interviewed in *The Guardian*, 14 November 1992.

24. Interview with Chief Constable Roger Birch, Sussex Constabulary, 9 July 1992.

25. Interview with Superintendent Mike Lewis, Sussex Constabulary, 9 July 1992.

26. Interviews with officers of Kent Constabulary, 12-13 November 1991.

27. Resolution of the European Parliament on the setting up of Europol (A3-0382/92), 22 January 1993, para.2.

Bibliography

Anderson M (1989) *Policing The World: Interpol and the Politics of International Police Co-operation.* Oxford: Clarendon.

Baker K (1992) 'Policing Europe, 1992'. Paper given to the European Chiefs of Police Conference: London.

Baldwin R (1987) 'Why Police Accountability?' *British Journal of Criminology* Vol. 32 pp.97-105.

Baldwin-Edwards M and Hebenton B (1992) 'European Policing and Data Protection Implications', ECPR Joint Sessions: Limerick.

Bentham K (1992) 'A European Police Council' in Anderson M and den Boer M (eds) *European Police Co-operation: Proceedings of a Seminar,* Edinburgh: European Police Co-operation Project.

Bigo D (1992) *The European Internal Security Field,* ECPR joint sessions: Limerick.

Birch R (1992) 'Why Europe needs Interpol' *Police Review* 17 January pp.120-121.

Bogdanor V and Woodcock G (1991) 'The European Community and Sovereignty', *Parliamentary Affairs,* Vol.44, pp.481-492.

Boys Smith S W (1992) 'Europe after 1992', Paper given to the European Regional Conference of the International Association of Chief Police Officers: Amsterdam

Brodeur J P (1983) 'High Policing and Low Policing: Remarks about the Policing of Political Activities', *Social Problems,* Vol.30 pp.507-520.

Brogden M (1987) 'The emergence of the police - the colonial dimension', *British Journal of Criminology,* Vol.32, pp.1-14.

Brogden M, Jefferson T and Walklate S (1988) *Introducing Policework* London : Unwin Hyman.

Bryant C (1991) 'Europe and the European Community', *Sociology* Vol. 25 pp.189-207.

Bulpitt J (1992) 'Conservative Leaders and the 'Euro Ratchet': Five Doses of Scepticism', *Political Quarterly*, Vol.63, pp.258-275.

Bunyan T (1991) 'Towards an authoritarian European state', *Race and Class*, Vol.32 pp.20-27.

Cain M (1979) 'Trends in the Sociology of Police Work', *International Journal of the Sociology of Law*, Vol.7 pp.143-167.

den Boer M (1991) 'Schengen: Intergovernmental Scenario for European Co-operation', Edinburgh: European Police Co-operation Project Working Paper.

den Boer M and Walker, N (1993) 'European Policing after 1992', *Journal of Common Market Studies* Vol.31 pp. 3-27

Dorn J, Murji S and South N (1992) *Traffikers: Drug Markets and Law Enforcement*, London: Routledge.

European Commission (1992) 'Abolition of Border Controls: Commission Communication to the Council and to Parliament', Com(92) 877: Brussels, 8 May.

European Commission (1993) 'Freedom of Movement in the Single Market, Background Report', ISEC/B5/93 Brussels, 10 February.

European Council (1992) 'European Council in Edinburgh', 11 12 December 1992: Conclusions of the Presidency.

Evans J S (1992) 'Europe after 1992', Paper given to the European Regional Conference of the International Association of Chiefs of Police. Amsterdam.

Federal Trust (1991) *Europe's Future: Four Scenarios*, London: Federal Trust for Education and Research.

Gallagher F (1992) 'Kent County Constabulary : its European Perspective' in Anderson M and den Boer M (eds) *European Police Co-operation: Proceedings of a Seminar.* Edinburgh: European Police Co-operation Project.

George S (1990) *An Awkward Partner: Britain in the EC*, Oxford: Oxford University Press.

Gilmore W C (1992) 'Introduction in Gilmore, W.C. (ed) *International Efforts to Combat Money Laundering*, Cambridge International Documents Series, Volume 4: Grotius.

Goldsmith A (ed) (1991) *Complaints Against the Police: The Trend to External Review*, Oxford: Oxford University Press.

Gorry P J (1991) *Evaluation of the European Unit*, MBA thesis: University of Warwick.

Gregory F (1992) 'Unprecedented partnerships in crime control; law enforcement issues and linkages between Eastern and Western Europe since 1989'. Paper given to the ECPR Joint Sessions. Limerick.

Gregory F and Collier A (1991) 'Cross Frontier Crime and International Crime - Problems, Achievements and Prospects with reference to European Police Co-operation', University of Southampton.

Grimshaw R and Jefferson T (1987) *Interpreting Policework: Policy and Practice in forms of Beat Policing*, London: Allen and Unwin.

Guyomarch A (1991) 'Problems of Law and Order in France in the 1980s: Politics and Professionalism', *Policing and Society* Vol.1 pp.319-332.

Halliday T C (1985) 'Knowledge Mandates: Collective Influence by Scientific, Normative and Syncretic Professions', *British Journal of Sociology*, Vol.36 pp.421-447.

Harding D (1991) 'On track for Europe', *Police International* Vol.1 No.10 pp.8-11.

Harrison A (1992) 'The Potential of Interpol as the Main Communications and Liaison Function for European Police Co-operation with Special Reference to Fraud' in Anderson M and den Boer M (eds) *European Police Co-operation : Proceeding of a Seminar.* Edinburgh: Edinburgh Police Co-operation Project.

HM Government (1991), 'The Government Reply to the Seventh Report from the Home Affairs Committee', Session 1989-90 HC 363-I, Cm 1367. London: HMSO.

HM Government (1992) 'Developments in the European Community: July to December', Cm 1857. London HMSO.

Holdaway S (1983) *Inside the British Police* Oxford: Blackwell.

Home Affairs Committee (1990) 'Practical Police Co-operation in the European Community', 7th Report 1989 90, HC 363 I. London: HMSO.

Home Affairs Committee (1992) 'Migration Controls at External Borders of the European Community: Minutes of Evidence'. 1991 92, HC 215. London: HMSO

Home Affairs Committee (1993) 'The Accountability of the Security Service': 1st Report 1992-93, HC 265. London: HMSO.

Hondius F (1992) 'Mutual Assistance between Business Regulatory Bodies: Multilateral Assistance in Europe', *Commonwealth Law Bulletin* vol.18, No.4.

House of Lords (1989) 1992: 'Border Controls of People', 22nd Report of the Select Committee on the European Communities, 1988-89, HL 90. London HMSO.

Jenkins J (1992) 'Jeux sans frontières' *New Statesman and Society*, Vol.5 No.226 30 October pp.22-23.

Jessop B (1990) *State Theory: Putting Capitalist States in their Place*, Cambridge: Polity.

Kendall R (1992) 'Interpol Today', *Policing* Vol.8 pp.279-285.

Kinsey R, Lea J and Young J (1986) *Losing the Fight against Crime*, Oxford: Blackwell.

Latter R (1991) 'Crime and the European Community after 1992' Wilton Park Papers No.31. London: HMSO.

McLaughlin E (1992) 'The Democratic Deficit: European Union and the Accountability of the British Police' *British Journal of Criminology* Vol.32 pp.473-487.

Manning P C (1977) *Police Work: The Social Organisation of Policing*, Cambridge, Mass.: MIT Press.

Mawby R I (1990) *Comparative Policing Issues: The British and American Experience in International Perspective*, London: Unwin Hyman.

Miles R (1993) 'Community Policing', *Computing* February 4.

Miller D (1992) 'Citizenship and European Union' ECPR Joint Sessions: Limerick.

Norman P 'Computerised Information Systems for Policing the Borders of the European Community', Liberty Working Paper.

Owers A (1993) *The Age of Internal Controls?*, London: Institute for Public Policy Research (publication forthcoming).

Punch M (1985) *Conduct Unbecoming*, London: Tavistock.

Raab C (1992) 'Data Protection: The European Dimension', ECPR Joint Sessions: Limerick.

Reiner R (1992), *The Politics of the Police*, (2nd ed.). Hemel Hempstead: Wheatsheaf

Reiner R (1991a) 'A Much Lower Pedestal', *Policing* Vol.7, pp.225-238.

Reiner R (1991b) *Chief Constables*. Oxford: Oxford University Press.

Reuss Ianni E and Ianni F (1983) 'Street Cops and Management Cops: The Two Cultures of Policing' in Punch M (ed) *Control in the Police Organisation*. Cambridge: Mass.: MIT (1983) pp. 251-274.

Riley L (1991) *Counter-terrorism in Western Europe: Mechanisms for International Co-operation*. MA Thesis: University of Essex.

Skolnick J (1975) *Justice Without Trial: Law Enforcement in Democratic Society* (2nd ed). California: John Wiley.

Spencer M (1990) *1992 and All That; Civil Liberties in the Balance*. London: Civil Liberties Trust.

Streeck W and Schmitter P C (1991) 'From National Corporatism to Transnational Pluralism: Organised Interests in the European Community' *Politics and Society* Vol.19 pp;133-164.

Terrill R J (1989) 'Organisation of Law Enforcement in the Soviet Union' in *Police Studies* Vol.12, pp.18-24.

Tindale S (1992) 'Learning to Love the Market: Labour and the European Community'. *Political Quarterly* Vol.63, pp.276-300.

Travis A (1993) 'Clarke winning fight over police revamp' *The Guardian* January 23.

TREVI (1991) 'The Development of Europol'. Report from TREVI Ministers to the European Council in Maastricht.

Tsimas K (1992) 'Draft Report on the abolition of controls at internal borders and free movement of persons within the EC'. Committee on Civil Liberties and Internal Affairs of the European Parliament: June 11.

van Outrive (1992a) 'Europol'. Committee on Civil Liberties and Internal Affairs of the European Parliament'.

van Outrive (1992b) 'Police co-operation'. Committee on Civil Liberties and Internal Affairs of the European Parliament.

van Outrive (1992c) 'The Entry into Force of the Schengen Agreements'. Committee on Civil Liberties and Internal Affairs of the European Parliament.

van Outrive (1992d) 'The setting up of Europol'. Committee on Civil Liberties and Internal Affairs of the European Parliament.

van Reenen (1989) 'Policing Europe after 1992: Co-operation and Competition' *European Affairs* Vol.3, No.2, pp. 45-53.

Walker N (1991) 'The United Kingdom Police and European Co-operation'. Edinburgh:. European Police Co-operation Project Working Paper.

Walker N (1992) 'Models of European Integration and Models of European Police Co-operation'. ECPR Joint Sessions: Limerick.

Walker N (1993) 'The dynamics of European Police Co-operation: the UK 'perspective' *Commonwealth Law Bulletin* (forthcoming).

Wilson J Q (1968) *Varieties of Police Behavior.* Cambridge, Mass. Harvard University Press.

Wren T (1992) 'The Enforcement of Confiscation Law in Great Britain' in *Action Against Transnational Criminality: Papers from the 1991 Oxford Conference on International and White Collar Crime.* London: Commonwealth Secretariat. pp.54-58.

CONCLUSIONS AND RECOMMENDATIONS
Robert Reiner and Sarah Spencer

Police accountability is now a moving target. As the chapters in this volume indicate, the ways in which the police are expected to be accountable have changed considerably in recent years and even more profound innovations are afoot. There are great dangers of wasting ammunition fighting yesterday's battles. In particular, the critical consensus for many years has focused on the problem of police independence. It has commonly been held that the police enjoyed too much freedom from legal and democratic checks, that they were 'out of control', a 'law unto themselves'. The import of developments in recent years, which the changes that are now being mooted by the Government will accentuate, is that the police at all levels are becoming more accountable and less autonomous. This enhanced accountability, however, is internal, managerial and increasingly centralised. Accountability to elected representatives at local level, supposedly a vital part of the tripartite system consolidated by the Police Act 1964, has withered on the vine (Reiner 1991). The anticipated restructuring which the Home Office appears to be seeking could destroy the vineyard altogether, as Barry Loveday's chapter shows.

The Home Secretary, Kenneth Clarke, announced on 23 March 1993 that he proposed to reduce the proportion of elected members on local police authorities from two thirds to one half, the balance comprising JPs and people appointed by him, with the chairperson also to be selected by the Home Secretary. Although he did not announce amalgamations, his statement to the Commons made it clear that these were in the offing. 'We may no longer need 43 separate headquarters maintaining 43 parallel organisations', he told MPs. Thus local forces could eventually be amalgamated into a small number of regional mega-forces, and local police authorities are to become half non-elected, undemocratic bodies consisting in part of appointees deemed worthy by central government. What little prospects people might now feel they have of influencing their local forces would disappear. In so far as effective policing depends upon public support and co-operation, these 'reforms' are likely to prove as counter-productive as they are undemocratic.

In many respects the present prospects for policing are chilling, threatening both the effectiveness and the legitimacy of the police. Their very radicalism, however, offers faint glimmers of hope because they will have destroyed some shibboleths which have hitherto blocked the prospects of democratic police accountability. Above all, the Government's current reforms will destroy the traditional doctrine of constabulary independence. In the past, governments have always staunchly defended it against local authority bids to influence policing policy, seeing its protection as a bulwark keeping politics out of policing.

Whilst the Government's proposals will leave untouched the legal responsibility of each individual constable for the exercise of legal powers in specific cases, they will mandate government control - not just *post hoc* exhortation - over law enforcement policy as well as the tight structuring of the discretion of the operational constable. This is because senior officers, from the chief constables of the large regional forces which are on the agenda to the superintendents in charge of 'local command units', are likely to be employed on relatively short-term contracts and subject to clearly spelt-out performance targets specified by central government and its appointees on local police authorities. Accountability of police commanders to the Home Office and its local nominees will thus not be of the *post hoc* 'explanatory' style which is the most that the current local police authorities enjoy. Police chiefs will have to follow the dictates of the centre, or join the workfare queues.

Rank-and-file constables could feel additional constraints on the exercise of their own traditionally vaunted discretionary powers, either because they too are on short-term contracts or because their managers will be anxious to extract the necessary performance from them. Thus the need to meet performance targets may destroy the mystical tradition of constabulary independence without having to breach its legal citadel.

It is ironic that the most cherished shibboleth of the British police tradition may be destroyed by a Conservative, law and order government in the name of managerial efficiency, after generations of radicals seeking this in the name of democracy have been successfully repelled. What is worrying about the Government's proposed police reforms is the technocratic and undemocratic spirit which animates them. Under the new regime, the police will be accountable as never before. Their priorities and goals will be fixed for them by outside bodies and failure to reach them will be sanctioned by performance related pay and ultimately by dismissal. The constable may not explicitly be told to arrest or prosecute 'this man or that one' (in Lord Denning's celebrated formulation of what the constabulary independence doctrine precludes)[1]; but decisions about arrest or the use of other law enforcement powers will inevitably be strongly influenced by the need to meet performance targets. It will pay the 'businesslike' police forces sought by Mr Clarke to pursue the government's business targets.

The doctrine of constabulary independence has always lacked any principled basis other than somewhat dubious judicial authority (Marshall 1965; Spencer 1985; Lustgarten 1986; Uglow 1988). We would certainly not argue for its resuscitation. The system which is to replace it, however, contains profound threats to both the legitimacy and the effectiveness of the police. This is because the bodies to which the police will be accountable at local level lack the representativeness and legitimacy which stem from election. Instead they will be dominated by appointees of the Home Office and magistrates (appointed by the Lord Chancellor). Unlike elected local authorities these cannot be ejected at the ballot box if they do not represent local opinion. Although the councillors on each authority will constitute 50 per cent, the balance will be determined by the chairperson chosen by the Home Secretary. The only other elected element in the system will be the Home Secretary, who is not necessarily accountable or responsive to local opinion.

This is thought not to matter because of a fundamental fallacy about the nature of policing which underlies government thinking. This is that policing decisions are primarily matters of neutral and technical expertise. What is needed is the right calibre of person - local business and professional people - who can speak for the supposed needs of their areas, and the expert views of central government civil servants and HM Inspectors of Constabulary. With the right management structures and technical know-how in place, efficient and effective policing will follow. What this technocratic picture neglects is the inevitably *political* character of most policing decisions, stemming above all from the fundamental nature of policing (Reiner 1992).

Policing is not about the delivery of a straightforward service to people demanding it. It is about the regulation of social conflict and the representation of social authority, through the use in the last resort of legitimate force. Policing is a largely coercive activity, even if physical force is comparatively seldom resorted to. Disputes about the appropriate priorities and styles of policing cannot be resolved by expertise alone. They are decisions about the purposes and justifications for getting some people to do what they do not want to do. Most police interventions are potentially the beginnings of the process of legal punishment, the delivery of a sanction to those whom it is deemed necessary to control or who are felt to merit retribution. It is for this reason that a liberal democratic society hems in the use of legal powers by the police with a set of legal restraints over their exercise. The social interest in law enforcement is balanced by the social interest in guaranteeing innocent people freedom from police interference and ensuring that those suspected of crime have reasonable opportunities to defend themselves. Thus, questions about the directions and methods of policing are not just technical ones but also political ones about the limits of state power and the nature of a society. Such questions must, like the law itself, ultimately be decided in a democracy by the electoral process (Lustgarten 1986).

Since most policing decisions primarily concern local matters, there must be an important role for local government. The involvement of local government is also necessary to balance the power of central government and of the professional police themselves. Because the police are the agency entrusted with the state's monopoly of legitimate force in its territory, it is vital that the control of policing is divided between different independent bodies to prevent a monolithic concentration of coercive power. Under the tripartite system, local government has provided part of the countervailing power, balancing that of central government and the police (although the power of local police authorities has been drastically weakened in recent years).

Locally, accountable policing is not just a matter of democratic legitimacy, however, but of effectiveness. Studies of how police clear up crimes show that successful detection is primarily the consequence of public co-operation (Reiner 1992 Ch.Four). The primary determinant of police effectiveness in dealing with crime is not managerial efficiency or technical prowess but the flow of information. The lifeblood of policing is public support. If sections of society are alienated from the police this is not only regrettable in itself but a serious barrier to the investigation of crime. To the extent that current government plans will decrease the possibility of local communities influencing policing through the ballot box they will undermine effective policing, no matter how rationally they reorganise management structures and expose police officers to dismissal for failing to meet targets.

Local committees dominated by the great and good chosen by central government cannot command the consent in particular of the least powerful, socially most marginal groups who may have the most information to offer to the police about high crime areas (Morgan 1989, 1992). While it can be argued that police authorities currently do not command such support, the solution cannot be to reduce number of elected representatives involved. It is vital to construct such channels of accountability as will inspire in all social groups the confidence that they *can* influence the police through the political process, and that policing is as much concerned with justice and legality as with attaining managerial performance targets.

The police reforms currently proposed by the government are double edged. They will make the police more accountable, but largely to central government and its appointees. In terms of Marshall's distinction between styles of accountability discussed in Reiner's paper, while police authorities will have to publish information on the achievement of performance targets, local people will lose the vestigial 'explanatory' accountability through the local authority which they enjoy now under the tripartite system. This will not be replaced by direct central government control in a 'subordinate and obedient' mode. The precise details of the strategy for attaining prescribed targets will be entirely the responsibility of the local police. But they will have to achieve centrally determined performance targets or suffer severe financial penalties and possibly the loss of their jobs. This amounts to a new mode of accountability, the 'calculative and contractual', which was not envisaged by Marshall. The crucial issues under it are who has the power to determine the targets, and assess whether they have been achieved. Under Mr Clarke's arrangements the answer is clear. The Home Secretary will.

This volume has tried to consider the principles upon which a democratic structure of police accountability should rest. This is necessary for a police system which enjoys public confidence and support and is thus capable of functioning effectively. By way of conclusion we will review these principles and how they may be implemented in a democratic, just and effective system of police accountability.

Police Accountability: the Fundamental Principles

The first paper considered the basic issues which must be tackled by a system of police accountability. *What type* of decisions do the police make (explicitly or implicitly) in exercising their powers? *To whom* should they be accountable for these different sorts of decisions? *What type* of accountability should they have? *What problems* are there in the effective achievement of police accountability?

The decisions made by the police differ fundamentally in terms of two dimensions which affect their accountability. Decisions may concern the output of police work: law enforcement or peace-keeping, the extent and style of use of police legal powers; or they may relate primarily to internal organisational matters. Decisions may also vary according to whether they relate only to specific individual cases or to general policies concerning whole classes of cases.

While decisions concerning internal organisational matters do raise significant issues with regard to accountability, the particularly controversial issues concern law enforcement decisions. The doctrine of constabulary independence has been articulated by the courts, the police and politicians over many years. It is the view that, in exercising legal powers in relation to the enforcement of criminal law, the constable enjoys an original authority under the Crown and cannot and should not be instructed by any outside bodies concerning the decisions made. The best way to enforce the law is a matter for the professional judgement of the constable and neither local nor central government can control it. This doctrine applies equally to the rank-and-file constable deciding how to handle a specific case, and to the chief constable deciding on the priorities and style of law enforcement for the force as a whole.

The constabulary independence doctrine lacks a firm basis in principle and derives primarily from suspicion about the integrity and capability of local government. Questions about law enforcement policy are ultimately political ones about the aims underlying the use of the power of the state. The final say in all political questions in a democracy must go to elected representatives. There is nothing about law enforcement issues which makes them qualitatively distinct in this regard. Nor should decisions in individual cases be ultimately sheltered from *post hoc* review by elected authorities. They should be able to instruct the police to act differently in similar cases in the future should they be dissatisfied with what was done.

What *is* peculiar about policing and law enforcement is their function of marking out the frontiers of social order and representing the legitimate authority of the state. It is particularly important that the power of the police organisation is not captured by a narrow partisan interest. This danger is not averted, however, by protecting the autonomy of the police from outside bodies. On the contrary this may act as a shield for the police to represent their own or some other partisan viewpoint. What is necessary to prevent a monolithic domination of policing by particular interests is a dispersal of power over police decision-making. The tripartite system in principle aims to do this, by dividing responsibility between local and central government, the professional police chiefs and the courts which can review the propriety of the exercise of powers by all three points of the triangle. The problem with the tripartite system has been the unbalanced distribution of power between its constituent elements. The local police authorities are being increasingly written out of the picture by case-law and practice since the 1964 Police Act (Reiner 1991, Loveday 1991).

We would not accept that there are any kinds of decision which should be shielded from external accountability on principle. However, police work in individual cases is particularly hard to review in practice, because of its low visibility to parties other than those immediately involved. This gives police constables a considerable measure of practical autonomy to frame acceptable accounts of unacceptable conduct (McConville, Sanders and Leng 1991). Whilst we would not preserve the constabulary independence doctrine in principle, the fact that it is peculiarly hard to affect police decision-making on the ground against the grain of police culture (Reiner 1992 Chap.Six) must be recognised. This raises particular problems for the construction of adequate mechanisms of accountability.

An Alternative Agenda

The structure of police decision-making and accountability should above all ensure that the power over police decision-making is not monolithic but divided between central government, local government and police officers themselves as the appointed officials. The responsibility of local government for ensuring that local services meet the needs and priorities of local people must be accepted if the essence of liberal democracy is not to be undermined.

Most policing issues concern only local areas, relating to small-scale crime and peace-keeping problems. Determining the objectives and priorities of this police work, and the allocation of resources, should be the responsibility of the locally elected police authority in conjunction with their chief officer of police. Ideally, police force boundaries should match local government areas. Within forces there would be local command units corresponding to current sub-divisions, as envisaged by the Audit Commission and HM Inspectorate. In order to encourage inter-agency crime prevention initiatives those responsible for local command units should work with councillors and officials on Community Safety Committees, as well as consulting their communities via consultative committees, meetings, surveys and other devices, organised by the police authority.

The local authority would have the primary responsibility for policing in its area with a general, and perhaps statutory, responsibility for law enforcement, crime prevention and community safety. These involve the activities of many other local agencies apart from the police, hence the proposal in Barry Loveday's chapter that they be co-ordinated by a Community Safety Committee. In this forum those responsible for planning and leisure facilities, for instance, would be obliged to confront the implications for crime of their proposals and to take alternative suggestions back to their respective committees before decisions were taken.

The purchaser/provider split now common in other public services should equally be reflected in the relationship between police authorities and the police. As Barry Loveday argues, a responsibility to purchase the service and thus to determine the service wanted and to monitor service delivery would for the first time enable police authorities to carry out the function they were given by the 1964 Police Act of ensuring the provision of an adequate and efficient force. Although chief constables would remain responsible for the daily running of their forces, they would have to work to general principles and policies decided together with the police authority, and in the light of the expressed wishes of the public as discovered by local consultation. In the event of disagreement about policy, chief constables would have to accept the police authority view in the final analysis, though they could of course try to persuade the authority that their view was preferable. If chief constables believed police authorities were acting for improper motives or illegally the matter could be referred to the Home Secretary and, failing agreement, to the courts. Chief constables would be unambiguously accountable to their police authority for implementing its policies. If reasonable attempts to reach agreement or improved performance had been tried and failed, the chief constable would be liable to dismissal. The courts could, of course, review the propriety of this. This is a clear breach of the traditional constabulary independence doctrine. The reorganisation being proposed by the present Government effectively destroys this in any event.

Our proposals offer accountability to elected representatives of local communities rather than appointed place persons, which must be preferable in terms of democratic legitimacy and public confidence. We also believe that elected authorities would be more responsive to a wide range of local opinion than an appointed body would. They should be concerned not only with output measures like arrest or clear-up rates but also with questions of legality and justice.

For such a system to work effectively, police authorities will need high quality management information. Mollie Weatheritt's chapter reviewed the great strides towards more adequate monitoring of police performance made in recent years by the HM Inspectorate of Constabulary, as well as bodies outside the police framework like the Audit Commission. These must be continued and built upon further. As she suggests, inspection reports should be written as lucidly as possible so that they can be used by the public and its representatives. They should strive to be analytical in approach, and aimed at enabling police authorities to carry out their functions. The involvement of lay people alongside police officers in the inspection process is a welcome development. This would be especially so if these were recruited from a broader social base than the established great and good who currently dominate bodies like the Police

Complaints Authority. It is also welcome that recent attempts by HMIC (and chief constables themselves) to measure performance have not been restricted to law enforcement or managerial efficiency indicators. Rather, they have aimed to develop indices of the quality and justice of the police service in a broader sense, including for example the reduction of race and sex discrimination. The quality of service initiatives can be welcomed, though we would replace their emphasis on meeting the targets of *consumers*, who are conceived as essentially passive individuals, with accountability to *citizens* who have the right to register their preferences through the political process.

The problem that has perennially bedeviled attempts at police reform has been the low visibility of everyday police work, which enables traditional police culture and practices to survive unscathed despite nominal changes in policy and organisation. Andrew Sanders' chapter tackles the thorny problems of influencing the practical exercise of police discretion. Certainly the rules governing police powers and legal procedures have to be as tight and unambiguous as possible. Whatever can be done to open up the backstage areas of police work should be attempted, by recording devices (including video as well as audio-taping of all areas of stations); lay visiting organised by police authorities, and perhaps civilianisation of the custody process. Rank-and-file opposition is likely to have the power to subvert any such measures, however, and it is necessary to try and win it over.

One possible strategy is to include co-opted rank-and-file members (through their representative bodies) on all policy making bodies (Goldsmith 1990). They could at least try to prevent by argument policies which would genuinely be unworkable or for other reasons quite unacceptable to operational police officers. This could have the effect of making the representatives part-owners of agreed policies, who would attempt to persuade those they represent of the reasons for them. The smaller the degree of alienation of the rank-and-file from policies, the less subversion would occur.

In the end, however, as Andrew Sanders argues, it is likely that investigating officers will inevitably experience themselves as frustrated in their efforts by rules protecting suspects' rights, even if they agree with their rationale in principle. The system willy-nilly places them in an adversarial position *vis-a-vis* suspects, and it is better to recognise this than wish it away. Imposing rules which prevent police officers carrying out the role which they have been given can result in them attempting to fulfil that role in other ways, and in less visible places. If it is unreasonable to expect police officers to see protection of the suspect as part of their role and to assist the innocent in their defence, defence lawyers must have greater powers, with rights of access to suspects as well as to all relevant records. The product of unlawful interrogations should be inadmissible in court and all confessions should require corroboration.

One principle we have argued for is the need for countervailing sources of power over policing decisions. The worst possible scenario is a monolithic concentration of the state's coercive power. This is one reason for our opposition to the enormous enhancement of Home Office power in present Government proposals. However, central government does have a number of vital roles to play in an adequate structure of accountability.

The functions of central government in our envisaged policing system would be four-fold. First, it would continue to provide central support services to all forces where there are economies of scale or other reasons why they cannot be provided locally on an efficient basis. These would include some training, particularly specialist and senior management training (where the numbers involved are too small for local schemes to be viable), research and development, forensic science facilities, and the Police National Computer.

Secondly, central government must have a role to play in setting national standards, for instance on what equipment should be used and the circumstances in which it can be used. This is necessary in order to ensure the compatibility of technology such as computers and radios when forces are working together, and to ensure that equipment is not used which would change the role of the police in a way which has not been authorised by Parliament. In that context, the Home Secretary significantly failed to answer an MP who asked whether his proposed new arrangements for devolved financial responsibilities to police authorities and chief constables would enable them to purchase the side-handed baton[2]. In our view, it is appropriate that local choice should be circumscribed to a limited extent by national standards of the kind we have suggested.

Thirdly, some operational policing functions are national matters and should be provided by national police units. These include diplomatic protection, anti-terrorist work and much of the security policing undertaken by Special Branch. There is also a growing volume of crime which is national and even international in scale. This has been the stimulus for the development of the National Criminal Intelligence Service (NCIS) which started work in 1992 and has the job of co-ordinating intelligence on serious crime, working with Regional Crime Squads and local CIDs as it has no operational role at present. It incorporates the work of several earlier more specialist national intelligence units, like the National Drugs Intelligence Unit and the National Football Intelligence Unit. In addition anxieties about the growth of international crime have fuelled the development of a number of European and international policing organisations, as outlined in Neil Walker's chapter. These include the Trevi and Schengen agreements, Interpol, and the new Europol proposed at Maastricht. As Neil Walker shows, the case for these has not been fully made out, but nevertheless they are clearly important developments. He also shows how these new forms of European or world policing in which the British police are increasingly involved lack even the rudimentary accountability structures of most domestic forces.

Little attention has been paid to the organisation and accountability of national policing units. Two distinct organisational models are available. The first is the present British pattern, where national units consist of officers seconded by local forces, though often commanded by a senior officer who has permanently left local policing in order to run the national unit. In theory such seconded officers remain locally accountable, though this is patently not achieved in practice. A second model is the recruitment of officers directly into national police units, as happens for example with the FBI in the United States. It would be likely that they would then clearly be seen as elite units, although the danger of this would be reduced if appointment to the unit was not for an officer's entire career but only for part of a career involving prior and subsequent posts in other forces. The advantage of the first model is that it might facilitate co-ordination with local forces, but the second would permit the recruitment of people into national specialist units who have specialist skills unnecessary for most local policing, such as knowledge of foreign languages. Whichever model is adopted, the crucial issue is for there to be a corresponding structure of accountability. We would suggest that the only feasible line of accountability is through the Home Secretary to Parliament, with regular scrutiny by the Home Affairs Committee. Although we considered the feasibility of a new National Police Authority, consisting of delegates from local police authorities, the Home Secretary, and representatives of the police staff associations, such a body would be unwieldy, could only meet infrequently, and would be unable to exercise the kind of policy direction and scrutiny of performance that is needed.

We do not in any sense envisage this national police unit (or units) being the precursor of a future national police force. We advocate it in acknowledgement of the fact that there are some policing activities and operations which do need to be organised at a national level. Recognising the desirability of the subsidiarity principle, that decisions should be taken by bodies as close as possible to those affected by the decision, we advocate strongly that the assumption be made that decisions will be taken, or operations controlled, by those responsible for a local command unit or force unless it is essential that they be taken at the national level.

The fourth role for central government is to monitor the efficiency and integrity of local forces. Just as local government is a necessary countervailing power against central domination of policing, so too the Home Office has to keep watch to prevent local tyrannies of the majority or use of the police for corrupt or partisan purposes. In addition the Home Office should monitor efficiency and attempt to spread good practice through its Inspectorate of Constabulary as at present, but with HMIC remodelled as suggested in Mollie Weatheritt's chapter. To represent the balance of local and national interests in policing, the present division of the burden of funding should continue, although we welcome the proposed relaxation of central controls over the use of funds allocated to local forces, subject to continuing auditing by the HMIC to assess value for money.

In sum, one of the virtues of the traditional British system of policing has been its finely tuned balance of local, central and professional control. In recent years this has become increasingly distorted by greater central control without any corresponding accountability for the policing role of central government. This has been associated with a disastrous decline in public confidence in and support for the police. The life-blood of effective policing, public co-operation and support, has been threatened. The present government's strategy of greater central control and the elimination of local government influence is not only undemocratic in principle. It is likely to be counter-productive and undermine the police effectiveness which it seeks to promote. This amounts to criminal damage against an institution vital for public security and national self-confidence.

Summary of Recommendations

1. That responsibility for police decision-making should be balanced between central and local government, and chief police officers, reversing the present trend towards effective central control.

2. That local police authorities should be entirely elected bodies without appointed magistrates or nominees from central government. Chief constables should be accountable to police authorities for meeting the objectives and performance targets

set by the authority and the Home Secretary. The local authority, of which the police authority should remain a part, should have responsibility for law enforcement, crime prevention and community safety in its area.

3. That police force areas should coincide with the boundaries of local government to help the public to identify with 'their' police force and avoid the weak accountability structure of Joint Boards or Joint Police Authorities.

4. That local command units should, as the Government intends, be responsible for service delivery according to the priorities and needs of their local community, but that responsibility for ascertaining local views should be that of the elected police authority, using consultative committees, surveys and other means. At local command unit level, councillors and officials responsible for services relevant to crime prevention should sit with the police on a Community Safety Committee to co-ordinate crime prevention initiatives.

5. Police authorities should be the purchasers of policing services and the police, except where the authority otherwise decides, the providers. Authorities should take responsibility for setting police objectives and performance targets and for monitoring the achievement of those targets; they must also have the authority to ensure that these targets are attained. It should be recognised that these developments will erode the much vaunted but unhelpful notion of constabulary independence while protecting the independent judgement of the officer in relation to particular acts of law enforcement.

6. In order to fulfil their responsibility for performance review, police authorities will need to have available to them the information which is currently being gathered internally for HMIC, the Home Office and Audit Commission. Those responsible for internal inspections should report to the Authority, as the body responsible for the police service, rather than those providing that service. Performance indicators should

reflect the priorities of the community, including, for instance, indicators of the treatment of suspects (such as access to solicitors) as well as, for instance, response rates to 999 calls.

7. In relation to law enforcement, vague offences should be redefined; evidence obtained in breach of PACE should be inadmissible and corroboration should be required for confession evidence. Back-stage areas of police work should be made more visible (eg. by recording devices, including video), lay visiting and perhaps civilianisation of the custody process. We should recognise that the police cannot be expected, in their adversarial role, to assist the innocent in their defence and therefore must provide defence lawyers with greater powers and resources to do so more effectively, including rights of access to suspects and to all relevant records. Complaints against police officers should be investigated by a genuinely independence body.

8. We have emphasised the need for elected police authorities to act as a countervailing power to central government, but the obverse is also true. Central government should, first, set national standards (eg. on equipment and the circumstances of its use); monitor the efficiency and integrity of local forces for which it will continue to provide most of the finance; and provide central services such as training.

9. The Home Secretary, and ultimately Parliament, should also take responsibility for the national police unit or units which should be established with operational responsibility for those policing tasks which reach across regional and national borders. Recognising the need for national planning and control of these functions, and creating a matching structure of accountability, would be preferable to the de facto national control exercised now with nominal and meaningless local accountability.

10. A national unit should take responsibility for liaising with European and international counterparts and advising the Home Secretary on legislative, policy and operational developments at the international level. National accountability must not,

however, be allowed to become a substitute for the accountability (with clear visible lines of decision-making) which is needed for the international decision-making bodies themselves, such as the Trevi group, and for Europol if and when it becomes operational. This must be to the appropriate bodies of the European Community and not only to national governments.

11. As the major developments in international policing are likely to be in the European context, these should be properly integrated within the EC as the institutional structure best equipped to co-ordinate a wide variety of programmes and most amenable to external scrutiny. In particular, the Europol organisation and the broader range of justice and Home Affairs matters, which represent a new 'pillar' of EC activity under the Treaty of Maastricht, should provide the centrepiece of international criminal justice efforts involving the UK. Further, the more detailed regulatory framework for Europol which emerges under the terms of the Treaty should involve both the national and the European Parliament in a general monitoring role and should extend jurisdiction to the European Court of Justice to safeguard individual rights.

Notes

1. In *R. v M.P.C. ex.p.Blackburn* 1968 2 Q.B. at p136

2. Commons Debate, 23 March 1993 col.778

Bibliography

Goldsmith A (1990) 'Taking Police Culture Seriously: Police Discretion and the Limits of the Law' *Policing and Society* 1:2.

Loveday B (1991) 'The New Police Authorities' *Policing and Society* 1:3.

Lustgarten L (1986) *The Governance of the Police* London: Sweet and Maxwell.

McConville M, Sanders A and Leng R (1991) *The Case for the Prosecution* London:Routledge.

Marshall G (1965) *Police and Government* London: Methuen.

Marshall G (1978) 'Police Accountability Revisited' in Butler D and Halsey A H (eds.) *Policy and Politics* London: Macmillan.

Morgan R (1989) 'Policing By Consent: Legitimating the Doctrine' in Morgan R and Smith D (eds.) *Coming to Terms With Policing* London: Routledge.

Morgan R (1992) 'Talking About Policing' in Downes D (ed.) *Unravelling Criminal Justice* London: Macmillan.

Reiner R (1991) *Chief Constables* Oxford: Oxford University Press.

Reiner R (1992) *The Politics of the Police* (2nd.ed) Hemel Hempstead: Wheatsheaf.

Spencer S (1985) *Called to Account* London: National Council for Civil Liberties.

Uglow S (1988) *Policing Liberal Society* Oxford: Oxford University Press.